Life Strategies
for Catholic Teens

Life Strategies for Catholic Teens

Tough Issues, Straight Talk

Jim Auer

Liguori

LIGUORI, MISSOURI

Imprimi Potest:
Richard Thibodeau, C.Ss.R.
Provincial, Denver Province
The Redemptorists

Published by Liguori Publications
Liguori, Missouri
www.liguori.org

Library of Congress Cataloging-in-Publication Data

Auer, Jim.
    Life strategies for catholic teens : tough issues, straight talk /
Jim Auer. 1st ed.
        p.   cm.
    ISBN 978-0-7648-1151-7
    1. Catholic youth—Religious life. I. Title.

BX2355.A925   2004
248.8'3'088282—dc22   2003065891

Printed in the United States of America
11 10   5 4 3

Contents

Introduction

If you're just joining us, this is live coverage on Channel 9 of the Division 1 State Finals championship title game. I'm Alicia McFarland, and with me here for a few moments is head coach, Duke Holwedge, of the Bishop Carson Crusaders. Coach, how does it feel to be here?"

"Fantastic, Alicia. The team's worked hard to get here, they're pumped up, we're ready."

"You've got a real challenge tonight. You're up against the team ranked not only number one in the state but number seven in the entire country. I assume that calls for some special strategies on your part. Can you give us any hint of how you're going to pull off an upset?"

"Strategy is everything, Alicia. We've been working on a lot of them, and I can tell you exactly what they are. Our first and most important strategy is do good. That's crucial—to do good."

"Uh...I'm sure you're right about that. Any other... strategies?"

"Absolutely. We're going to score points—*more* points than the other team."

"Well, right again, I'm sure, Coach. Do you have a... strategy for accomplishing that?"

"Absolutely. We're going to keep them from scoring very many points."

Makes you wonder how the Crusaders ever made it to the finals, doesn't it? You need better planned and more finely tuned strategies than "do good" to win a game—and to live as a Catholic Christian in life. Without them, we're "feathers in a wind." I like that. Reminds me of the line from Queen's great classic, "Bohemian Rhapsody": "Any way the wind blows...doesn't really matter to me." And we all know how tragically that rock ballad ends.

There's only one author's name on this book, but in a very real sense there should be a lot more—the names of the several thousand teens I've taught. Some of them are extremely old now, like in their early forties. Others are still in their mid teens.

The ideas for writing this book have come from teaching them; from talking with them, listening to them, and getting glimpses into their lives; from caring and sometimes worrying about them; from rejoicing with them over happy stuff, and from occasionally getting my shirt wet with tears created by painful stuff. Different ones have operated on different life strategies (or, sometimes, on none), and that has had a lot to do with how their lives have turned out.

It's based on what's important to you—the things we sometimes call "values to live by." Maybe for some class or other you've had to make a list of ten things that are really important to you. It's the kind of assignment teachers like to give because it seems as though it will lead to a lot of interesting discussion. Sometimes it does, especially if somebody puts something on his/her list like "giant squids" or "nasal health" and means it.

Sometimes we give the "right" answers, we mean them, and we do our very best to live by them each day— God, faith, family, love, friendship, honesty, truth, and so forth. Sometimes we give those same right answers, sort of mean them, but live otherwise, spending most of our time and energy in the pursuit of pure pleasure, excitement, cool social status, money for the sake of money, and so forth. Often we're a mixture.

What's important to you?

What's important *about* you—you on the inside, you as a person, not just your cute nose?

When you look outside of yourself at life, at how you interact with other people, how you handle challenges and an assortment of possibilities, what do you make your decisions by?

I guess that's enough of an introduction, enough to get us started thinking about life strategies. Besides, this is a good stopping point because the dog is practicing an excellent strategy for her life: enter office, bark, place paw on my knee, then lie down, roll over, wag tail, and look hopeful.

Works every time.

Of course, her life is pretty simple, and all she wants right now is to be petted and perhaps have me throw a little soccer ball so she can chase it.

Your life isn't that simple, and you want more than that, even if you play soccer. You need some deeper strategies.

ONE

You're Worth Taking Care Of

Or do you not know that your body is a temple of the Holy Spirit within you, which you have from God, and that you are not your own?

–*1 Corinthians 6:19*

Thanks to oldie radio stations, many teens can sing or lip-sync oldie lyrics better than the "old folks" who grew up with those songs. You may be one of them. Here's a test.

"It's my party and I'll ___ ___ ___ ___ ___."

Very good. Now here's a bigger challenge. These lyrics are older than oldies. They're pre-Elvis, pre-Chuck Berry, pre-Platters.

"Button up your overcoat / When the wind blows free / Take good care of yourself / ___ ___ ___ ___."

Now the last word has to rhyme with "free," right? "I

want you to live to be ninety-three" works for the rhyme, but there's an overload of syllables. "Or I'll flatten thee" works for both rhyme and rhythm, but it kind of departs from the spirit of the previous lyrics. Another hint: The first two words are "You belong."

"To me"—excellent.

My wife must have heard those lyrics in her youth. She applies them frequently to me. It's a good thing; thanks to her, I'm alive to write this book. My problem is not remembering to zip my jacket when it's windy. My problem is food. Not how much, but what.

If I followed my taste buds, I would eat four or five eggs every morning, a thick burger or ham sandwich every noon, and a thick slab of beef every evening. My taste buds' idea of health food is to slip a little lettuce on the burger between the cheese slices. For someone my age, this is like saying, "I want to meet my Maker *soon*!"

My wife, Rose, realizes this. She sees me eyeing the carton of eggs and speaks soft, gentle words of persuasion, such as "Don't even think about it." She always adds, "I want you around for a long time."

The words *Take good care of yourself / You belong to me* are from an old-fashioned love song. But they could also be spoken by a parent to his or her child. That includes God speaking to each of us. No matter how independent we start to feel, we belong to God. It's that simple, and nothing we do will ever change it. Taking good care of ourselves is not self-centered. It's actually a duty: we belong to God, and God doesn't want his belongings trashed or neglected.

Few people would disagree with the idea of caring for themselves. Deciding what that means, however, isn't always easy. Many impostors and pretenders try to claim the role of "taking care of yourself." Here are a few of them.

- *Surrounding and filling yourself with as many pleasures, thrills, and good times as possible.* A lot of movies and TV series make this look like the best possible lifestyle. Few of them show the truth—that this lifestyle can leave you unhealthy, addicted, and pregnant. Or all of the above.
- *Always (or wherever possible) putting your own interests ahead of everyone else's.* No. That's contrary to the life of service that Jesus taught and modeled. It indicates not having grown out of an emotional baby bed.
- *Making your life as easy as possible by removing or ignoring as many obligations as possible.* No again. That's deliberately wasting your gifts and making a goal out of nonachievement. It might also be called slobbitude.

We'll look at five areas of our lives—body, mind, feelings, relationships, and spirit—and talk about some of the ways to take good care of yourself in each, along with identifying some further impostors.

Body

Imagine someone who decorates the outside of his or home every season with glitzy, attention-getting stuff. A three-thousand-light display at Christmas. Dozens of lighted Halloween pumpkins and skeletons. Inside the house is a recreation room with a state-of-the-art entertainment center.

But this person doesn't fix leaky plumbing, never has the furnace cleaned, ignores thumping sounds from the hot water heater, and figures that water leaking into the basement through cracks in the foundation will someday just stop.

Not intelligent. But sometimes we're a little like that. We spray, powder, and deodorize our bodies. We put stuff on our skin to make it look terrific. We wear cool clothes. We buy and enjoy things that look good, sound good, taste good, and feel good. But we don't always pay enough attention to what we're doing to the *inside* of our bodies.

We could make a standard horror list of illegal substances, but you've heard about them since your first drug-awareness program at school, which was probably back in primary grades. You know what they are, and it's usually no problem to get them if you want them. But it's easy for a young body to *seemingly* get away with them for a while.

It's easy for a young body to get away with a lot of things for a while simply because it's young. Besides things on the list of illegal substances, that includes perfectly legal things like an excess of calorie-infested doughnuts and junk food, a lack of sleep, and a lack of exercise.

Be good to your body in all ways—besides simply making it look good.

Mind

In this life, our bodies and our minds are so closely connected that taking good care of the body is, in many ways, part of taking good care of the mind. The mind functions a lot better when the body has had enough sleep, for example, and isn't dependent on chemicals.

There's another similarity. An important part of caring for the body has to do with what we put into it. The same is true of the mind. "What am I putting into my mind?" is an excellent self-check question we should all ask now and then.

I'm not talking about things like history notes, chemistry formulas, and verb forms. They may feel like toxic mental substances at times, but they're not going to cause decay. I'm talking about things that have the power to form attitudes toward people and attitudes about life. The things we deliberately watch, listen to, and hang around have that power, whether we realize it or not. We can try to be cool and claim we're so independent that none of that stuff rubs off on us, but that's self-deception.

For example, indulging in frequent doses of pornography eventually destroys the idea of sex as a beautiful, private expression of love between a husband and a wife.

The same is true of frequent exposure to media that portray sex basically as a comedy or a pleasure ride to which we're entitled.

Self-deception is easy. A local newspaper columnist wrote an antipornography column that stirred up quite a debate, and the paper printed some of the responses from readers. One man wrote, "I own between 300 and 400 porn videos, but it's not like I'm obsessed with them or anything." That would be laughable if it weren't so tragic.

It's not possible to ingest a daily diet of angry rap lyrics that portray violence as a normal action or reaction and still become a happy, peaceful person who recognizes the beauty of this world and tries to make it a better place. That's like standing in a cloud of grimy soot and not getting any on you. True, some lyrics point out deep social problems, and that needs to be done. But pointing out social problems along with heavy doses of rage and threat does nothing to solve them and does a lot to keep them going.

Feelings

Taking good care of your feelings involves finding out what they are (not always as easy a job as it sounds) and then asking yourself whether you're handling them or they're handling you.

A good self-check question here is, "What *do* I most commonly feel?" Put names to them. If your answer is "almost nonstop happiness, contentment, confidence, legitimate pride, and fulfillment," then you're in great shape. You're also a little unusual.

If your honest answer contains a lot of things like doubt, stress, anger, resentment, and worry, then there's some work to be done, and you could probably use some help doing it. A school counselor is a good start.

For some reason, many people think that seeing a counselor amounts to admitting they're too weak to handle life. That's a lot of…stuff you find in a farm field.

People enlist help with other aspects of life and don't feel stupid about it. They attend seminars to learn how to run a business better, they take singing and acting lessons, they pay a golf pro to help them improve their game. They seek help in just about any area of life that's important to them. But when it comes to seeking help with handling feelings and life in general, suddenly that has a bad image.

It shouldn't. If your feelings are handling you instead of vice versa, find someone to help you deal with them. That's not weak; that's smart. It's part of taking good care of yourself.

Relationships

A few people apparently are cut out to be hermits and are quite happy living by themselves. If you're not one of them, then you have interactive relationships with other people. As with feelings, still another good self-check question is, "Am I handling my relationships or are they running me?"

Few relationships are problem free. In fact, a problem-free relationship is probably so distant that we could hardly call it a relationship at all. Getting through and past difficulties is precisely one of the ways a relationship grows stronger and healthier.

A good relationship challenges us to give, to become more flexible, less self-centered. It should broaden us, enrich us, and open us to new experiences, to new ways of seeing things.

But when the giving becomes one-sided, when the demands and expectations are almost always on us and seldom on the other person, then the relationship has become *ownership*, and that's not good. Or when the new experiences and new ways of looking at things make us uncomfortable, when we're doing them reluctantly and only to avoid ending the relationship completely, that's not good either.

At this moment, thousands of people are living in nice surroundings, holding good jobs, enjoying life, and they wouldn't be there without the help of the relationships they chose. Likewise, thousands of people are living in prison cells and other less-than-nice places, and they wouldn't be there without the "help" of the relationships they chose, either.

Taking good care of yourself includes choosing and strengthening relationships that are genuinely good for everyone involved.

Spirit

Long ago, Saint Augustine wrote, "You have made us for yourself, O God, and our hearts are restless until they rest in you."

For brief or even lengthy periods, we can operate as if that were not true. We can distract ourselves with activities and pleasures and career pursuits and hundreds of other things, but if there's no "God stuff" in our lives, an emptiness exists that can grow almost like a cancer, like a black hole swallowing up the other things and turning them empty, too. Problem is, we often don't see it or realize it at the time.

God is big. In the end, we need to make God big in our lives. Taking good care of ourselves includes taking care of the one thing that in the end means more than anything else. Some people find that a little scary, because it seems as if paying a lot of attention to God will crowd out other things, especially the fun things, in their lives.

But I've never heard anyone say, "Yeah, I used to have fun, used to really enjoy life. But then I let God into my life in kind of a big way. Spoiled most of the good times. Gosh, I sure miss 'em."

Whether it means paying more and better attention to your diet, your lifestyle, your relationships—or even buttoning up your overcoat—God tells us, "Take good care of yourself...you belong to me."

Words From the Word

But we have this treasure in clay jars, so that it may be made clear that this extraordinary power belongs to God and does not come from us.

–2 Corinthians 4:7

Other Voices

This above all: to thine own self be true / And it must follow, as the night the day / Thou canst not then be false to any man.

–Shakespeare, Hamlet, Act 1, Scene 3

All along, I thought I was looking out for me. Well, I sort of was, but not in a good way, I was just giving myself thrills, being a big (_____). I have to learn what looking out for me really is. And right now I'm scared about learning that.

–Aaron, 22, currently incarcerated,
soon to be released; pray for him

Bottom Line

Our entire being—our bodies, our feelings, our minds, everything about us—is a gift from God to be used as well and as wisely as we can. We need to recognize this gift and take good care of it.

TWO

Loving Yourself...
For All the
Right Reasons

You shall love your neighbor as yourself.

–Matthew 22:39, Leviticus 19:18

Your eyes beheld my unformed substance. / In your book were written all the days that were formed for me, / when none of them as yet existed.

–Psalm 139:16

I've been going with this incredible girl for well over three decades. We've been married for thirty-five years. We've had some tough times here and there, but overall, to rephrase the country song, loving her has been easier than anything I've ever done.

I've been with this other person too for, let's see…well, it's a lot more than three decades. We didn't decide to get together. The relationship was prearranged, no choice about it.

I'm supposed to love this person also, but it's usually harder than loving my wife or my children. Some days I get along with this person fairly well. Other times, I'd like to change this person so I could get along with him better.

Me.

What about you? Do you like yourself…love yourself?

"Do you love yourself?" sounds like a very strange question. It invites a couple of very different answers.

One is, "Well, of course—obviously! How could I not love somebody as cool as I am? It's that loving other people stuff (especially some I could mention in particular) that gets difficult."

True enough on the second point. Loving other people is not always easy. Actually, it's often difficult. Actually, it's often maddening. Actually, it often requires asking for the grace of God to do so because on our own, we're too upset to do so. There have been times when I have had to ask for the grace to love people who had an endless stream of excuses for missing assignments and who developed a stomach virus on test days.

But loving yourself is also a big challenge, and many people have a hard time with it. I've even heard kids say, "I hate myself." I learned not to say, "Oh, you don't really mean that," because (hopefully only temporarily) it may have been true. I'd sometimes give them a hug and say, "Well, nasty, awful, hateful people deserve a hug too." It didn't make the problem vanish, but it usually got a grateful grin.

The second reaction is, "Loving *yourself?* That's weird!"

No, it's not. Well, I guess if every time you looked in the mirror, you leaned over, gave yourself a big kiss, and said, "You sweet, adorable creature," that would be on the strange side. And, in fact, as we'll see below, that's not true love of self.

There are some differences between loving yourself and loving another person. But there are also a surprising number of similarities.

First, let's bring out the proof that this love of self is absolutely legitimate and healthy. And you don't get any better proof of anything than something said by our Lord. He was very big on loving others, as you may have heard just a time or two now and then here and there.

But when he expressed this as a commandment, he said, "You shall love your neighbor as yourself." That's *"as yourself."* Not *"instead of yourself"* or even *"much more than yourself."*

I've met (and sometimes taught) people whose neighbors would have ended up bloody if they had been "loved" in the same way those people "loved" themselves.

Of course, Jesus was basing this comparison on healthy self-love. So what is that? And what are some of the things that may look like it but aren't? Let's start with the second question and sweep out the impostors by examining some things that definitely are not genuine love of self.

It's not self-worship, which puts self first in everything and at the center of everything, because, after all, *they deserve it!* Everything they do is wonderful; and even if it isn't truly wonderful, it's reasonable; and even if it isn't reasonable, it's explainable. They make no mistakes, and even if they do some little tiny thing that may somehow *seem* like a mistake to other people, it certainly isn't their fault.

They feel they deserve the very best rewards that the universe has to offer simply because of who they are. "I exist. More than that, I breathe. More than that, I get out of bed in the morning. And all through it, *I am me—therefore, I am owed.*"

Psychologists call this an unrealistic "sense of entitlement." Spiritual writers might call it worshiping a false god. Old-time grandmas called it being a spoiled, obnoxious brat.

This "sense of entitlement" is, unfortunately, extremely easy to absorb almost without realizing it in our culture. Every day, to use just one example, dozens of companies try to persuade you that you both need and deserve a wireless, hand-held gadget that gives you high speed Internet connection; enables you to communicate with other people through voice mail, text messaging, picture taking, editing, and forwarding; plans your day for you, reminds you of appointments, and almost tells you it's time to go potty. Do these things make life better? Maybe.

Depends on how much time you pour into them doing things that really don't have to be done—time that maybe ought to go somewhere else. Do you absolutely *need and therefore deserve* one of these things? Of course not.

Loving yourself is not conceit, either. A conceited person looks at almost everyone else and thinks, "I'm glad I'm better than they are."

Jesus illustrated conceit in his parable of the Pharisee and the tax collector. "The Pharisee, standing by himself, was praying thus, 'God, I thank you that I am not like other people: thieves, rogues, adulterers, or even like this tax collector'" (Lk 18:11).

It's easy to hear that parable and think, "Gosh, I'm glad I'm not like that Pharisee. He was so stuck up and superior. I would never pray a conceited prayer like that" —which is *exactly the attitude the Pharisee's prayer illustrates!* True, probably none of us would put the attitude into an actual prayer. But it doesn't have to be verbalized in an actual prayer in order to be conceit. "I'm glad I'm not like *those* people" qualifies very well.

True self-love is not excessive pampering. It doesn't mean seeking out every comfort, taking a fifteen-minute break after five minutes of work, feeling you have a positive right to sleep in until early afternoon every weekend, trying to get results for little or no effort, or buying yourself the latest and best of everything and feeling horribly deprived if you don't own one of those hand-held wireless devices we mentioned earlier.

Finally, self-love is not an endless series of excuses for mistakes, faults, irresponsibility, nonachievement, or just plain wrong stuff. Automatic, all-the-time reactions of "I couldn't help it," "It wasn't my fault," and "Well, I only did that because…" are signs of self-deceit, not self-love. Is it ever true that something was not your fault? Absolutely! Always? Reality check needed.

So, what *is* self-love—the real kind?

True self-love is based on accepting God's opinion of you. Your conception may have been elaborately planned, or it may have been accidental in one way or another. But to God, you are no accident. God saw you back when big dinosaurs were dining on little dinosaurs. God saw you when the Big Bang, if it happened, was just starting to rumble a little. And God *loved* what he saw.

Let's think about this "God loves me/you" stuff because in a lot of ways we're screwed up on it.

Have you ever thought something like this? "Well, sure, God loves me, yeah, I know that, God loves everybody, so God loves me because it's…well, it's in his job description! *He has to love everybody, including me—he's God! That's his job!*"

That's about as true as saying you *have to* order mushrooms on your pizza just because it's on the menu in front of you. If you like mushrooms, you'll choose to order them. If you don't, you won't. Simple. But you're in charge of your pizza.

Well, God is in charge of God's people and God's universe, and God doesn't *have* to do *anything*. It's one of the perks of being God. God does what he does because God *chooses* to do so. Totally, completely, freely *chooses*. Nobody tells God, "Now, come on, you know you have to do this, or at least you really ought to." God doesn't do something because it's on the list "Things I Have to Do This Millennium."

God considers you immensely lovable. Even if you yourself and ten thousand other people don't, hopefully, that's not your situation. Don't argue. *Don't argue!* God's opinion isn't going to change (even against the objections of yourself and ten thousand other people, which, as we said, hopefully is not the case).

But it's okay to ask why.

Now we could consult a dozen manuals of theology and find quotes in them, but this will probably work better. Answer this question: Are you going to love your kids? Even when they mess up? Even if they ignore you for a while? Even when they display an enormous lack of talent at something?

Of course you will. You'll look at your kids and see parts, reflections, of yourself, and you will choose to love and care for those reflections even if they're off somewhere goofing around, not even thinking about you. This doesn't mean you'll love and approve of everything they do, but you *will* love *them*.

God is like that. And God is a whole lot better at it than we are.

So loving yourself is based on the one thing that does not change no matter what you do or what happens in your life: You are God's child, a reflection of God, whether you're reflecting clearly or muddily. And that's all it takes.

You may have a ton of great qualities and talents. You may be popular, athletic, creative, and artistic—and even have a cute nose on top of it all. And it's fine to feel satisfaction in any of those things. On the other hand, you may *not* possess all of those qualities, and the ones that you do have can change or fade. The foundation of what makes you worthwhile (and therefore lovable, even to yourself) is that you are God's child. That fact will never change. You need to hang on to that whenever, and for whatever reason, you've sunk toward the bottom of your "List of Lovable People."

Here are some things that can lead you to put yourself to the bottom of that list, and keep you from loving yourself honestly and realistically.

- *Guilt over a past big mistake.* You might benefit from talking about this with someone you trust, but in the meantime, you can help yourself out with a big dose of "That was then, this is now." Jesus said he had come to call sinners, not people who were already righteous.

  Trying to excuse a past mistake in a cowardly manner and avoiding responsibility for it is one thing. Being kind to the person who made it (in this case, yourself) is another. They're just not the same thing.

- *Past abuse.* Feelings of being used or of being damaged material can hang around for a long time, and a person deserves some professional help to work through these feelings. But anyone who has been abused in any way needs to know that having been used for cheap purposes does not change a person's value. A diamond necklace that's temporarily used as a door chain is still a diamond necklace.

- *Feeling you don't measure up.* Meeting some standard of achievement or working toward it is a great thing as long as the yardstick measures something both *worthwhile* and *possible.* But attempting too much too soon in any area can send you into a downer when great success doesn't happen quickly.

  Make sure that the area in which you want to measure up is something that will really matter throughout most of your life. If you're popular for good reasons, enjoy the situation. If, for whatever reason you're not, remind yourself that the business, sports, and entertainment worlds are full of people who were nowhere near the top (or even the middle) of the social ladder during their teen and young adult years. And don't compare yourself to people who don't really exist—for example, the "physically perfect" people playing sand volleyball in an advertisement photograph that's been computer enhanced a couple dozen ways.

All this is easy for an adult to say. And I know that it hurts when you seem to fall short of some success that you very much want. That doesn't feel good at any age. But don't let it lead you to think less of yourself or to love yourself less. There will always be people who are smarter than you are, more popular than you are, more athletic than you are, wealthier than you are, more something-or-other than you are.

Many of the things you do when you truly love others apply to loving yourself. For example, you don't insist that they be perfect. You forgive their faults and imperfections. You don't hold grudges over things they did that may have caused you hurt at one time. You don't abandon them when times are tough. You're willing to start over. You try to get to know them on the inside and understand where they're coming from. You give them a push and even a loving correction when they need it. You don't give them things that are bad for them, and you don't look the other way when they're about to do something that could bring them harm.

When love is real, it doesn't depend on externals or a purely emotional rush. You simply love the person for who he or she is and try to meet his or her real needs. A good example is someone who cares for a spouse or a friend who is disabled. Real love of self is like that. It doesn't depend on the externals of appearance or popularity. It doesn't depend on the rush of scoring a winning run or shooting a key basket.

You love yourself because you're God's kid. Simple as that.

Words From the Word

> See what love the Father has given us, that we should be called children of God, and that is what we are.
>
> *−1 John 3:1*

> For it was you who formed my inward parts; / you knit me together in my mother's womb. / I praise you, for I am fearfully and wonderfully made.
>
> *−Psalm 139:13–14*

Other Voices

> Consult not your fears but your hopes and your dreams. Think not about your frustration, but about your unfulfilled potential. Concern yourself not with what you tried and failed in, but with what is still possible for you to do.
>
> *−Pope John XXIII*

> Every saint has a past and every sinner a future.
>
> *−Russian proverb*

Bottom Line

Genuine self-love is not self-worship and has nothing to do with being self-centered. Quite the opposite—it's based on being God-centered and seeing your immense value as a child of God. It's likewise necessary for living an emotionally healthy life.

THREE

How to Be Stunningly Beautiful

Ah, you are beautiful, my beloved, truly lovely.

–Song of Solomon 1:16

E very year, *People* magazine publishes an issue fea-
turing "The Fifty Most Beautiful People" in the
country. Chances are, I won't be featured this year. Or
any year. Don't laugh too hard. Chances are, neither will
you.

Of course, we could work at it. We could enlist a lot
of help, at least if we had enough money. Let's start with
the face. Did you know there are at least two hundred
thirteen varieties of products to make your face beautiful? And that does *not* include makeup!

Two hundred thirteen is the number I counted in Aisle
5-B of a large discount drugstore one day. An even larger
store may carry more. Toners, astringents, moisturizers,

deep-pore cleansers, therapeutic lotions, cleansing gels, facial masks and scrubs, and an army of oil, acne, and blemish fighters...you get the idea.

Remember that these products did not include makeup and they addressed only the face. They did not include all-purpose skin lotions or products to make hands and feet look beautiful. There's probably a product (or maybe a dozen) designed to create or enhance elbow and ear-lobe beauty.

There's nothing wrong with having beautiful earlobes, a beautiful face, or even beautiful kneecaps, for that matter, as long as you don't get obsessed with it. But it's not the only kind of beauty. Those things are outward beauty, the stuff that makes magazine covers and calendars.

If you have that beauty to whatever degree, as society would measure it, wonderful. Be grateful. This chapter isn't going to make the point that it has no value, or that truly good and holy people have absolutely no interest in looking attractive.

But there's also inward beauty, something that can't be produced, encouraged, or enhanced by anything that comes in a bottle, a tube, a jar, a spray can, or a soap bar. Inwardly beautiful people possess certain traits. Here are a few.

- *Beautiful people give themselves.* They say things such as "I'll take care of that for you." "Is there anything I can do?" "I'll help" (even if they're busy), "What do you need?" "I'll drive you there." "If you'd like me to take care of the decorations, I've got some time." "I can stop by the store on my way home." Sometimes they don't even ask. If it's plain that something needs to be done, they simply do it.

They don't ask for great recognition for doing these things, either. They appreciate a thank-you, but they don't seek hero medals. Just being able to give and to help is satisfaction enough. That's what separates them from people who routinely see the same needs and think, *Not my problem* or *What do I get if I take care of this?*

- *Beautiful people accept others without judging them...and without changing their own values and standards.* They don't get trapped in stereotypes, labels, and prejudices. They talk to the homecoming queen, as well as to the shy girl who doesn't wear cool clothes because her family is struggling and can't afford them. They're friendly and respectful to the classmate who gets teased for being religious, and they're friendly and respectful to the classmate who does a joint before school and another one afterward. Chances are they worry about the latter and perhaps pray for him or her.

- *Beautiful people build.* In particular, they build up other people. They boost, bolster, and energize the way other people feel about themselves. You come away from them feeling that you're a valuable, capable person. They build their own self-esteem by helping others build and strengthen theirs. They know that when everyone feels included and appreciated, life is fun. They know that exclusion and put-downs don't make life happier or genuinely more fun for anybody.

- *Beautiful people are peacemakers.* That makes sense, of course, because peace is beautiful and war is ugly. They hurt when they see someone harming someone else. They ache when they see people attacking one another, whether the weapons are knives, fists, words, accusations, gestures, facial expressions, or deliberate ignoring.

  They try to bring people back together, even when they sometimes get hurt in the attempt. They don't take sides, but they're not afraid to say firmly that a particular action is wrong.

- *Beautiful people see and appreciate beauty.* They're amazed at the variety of colors, shapes, and textures of flowers. They watch a puppy romping around a yard or hear toddlers giggling, and they connect these things with the joy that God placed in being alive. They see one kind of beauty in the smooth, glowing skin of the newborn and another in the dry, wrinkled skin of the aged. Like Jesus, they see the hurting beauty even in the sinner who wants to stop messing up but hasn't yet found or accepted the strength to do so.

- *Beautiful people forgive.* When someone hurts them, they suffer just like anybody else. But they don't cling to their anger and seek revenge. They know that joy, peace, and growth come with simple forgiveness—and they know from experience that "simple" does not mean "easy." They know the difference between forgiving and allowing themselves to be repeatedly victimized and treated badly. They realize that continued outrage, fuming, and soaking in emotional vinegar will only make their lives unsettled and unhappy.

- *Beautiful people have something called "character."* That's a little difficult to define. *Webster's New World Dictionary* lists sixteen definitions of "character" used as a noun. Number 8 says, "moral strength; self discipline, fortitude, etc."

  "Moral strength" means that doing the right thing is more important than any profit, advantage, or pleasure that might be gained from doing the wrong thing. People with character operate that way even when it isn't easy, even when they take heat for it, even when it means doing without something they would like to have.

  There's a good reason for the "etc." in Webster's definition # 8 of "character." Character includes the items listed and much more. I personally would add this: "not being like Silly Putty."

Silly Putty is great stuff. If you don't have any, you should invest in some, along with a jar of bubble fluid, and relive part of your childhood.

Remember how Silly Putty eventually takes the shape of whatever container you store it in? Well, that's fine for Silly Putty—but not for people. "Silly Putty People" sooner or later brainlessly take the shape of (meaning, go along with, think like, act like) whatever group of people they're with.

People of character decide if and to what extent they want to be like the social environment they're in, and they take their own shape based on what they know is right.

One of the most beautiful people I ever knew was "Heavy." His real name was Arthur, but he was Heavy to everybody including himself because of his size—about three hundred wonderfully black, African-American pounds. You can't weigh inward beauty, but if you could, I don't think there's a scale large enough to handle the task of weighing Heavy's inward beauty.

He was in the restaurant business for more than four decades. He owned and ran "Heavy's Place" in a part of Cincinnati which was definitely *not* where the rich people lived or gathered or even wanted to visit. He cooked the food, frequently served it, and did a lot of the cleaning up. The menu at Heavy's Place featured dishes you won't find at any franchise or even at most restaurants with extensive menus.

But the food was only part of it. Heavy served about as much help and hope as he did food.

If you could pay for your meal, or part of it, you were expected to do so. But if you were down to your last fifty cents (people in the neighborhood sometimes were), you would still get a full meal at Heavy's. He would put your name at the top of a page in an old notebook and record the price of the meal. You were expected to repay the debt...when you could. He never counted the days until that happened or attached any interest to the loan.

People who are now adults remember growing up in the neighborhood and being able to go to school with paper and pencils and decent clothes because of loans that Heavy made.

He worked the restaurant until he was almost seventy, sometimes sixteen hours a day, Monday through Saturday. He came to work for one reason: to make people happy and hopeful. He wanted to make money for one reason: to give it away.

He should have made *People*'s list of "Beautiful People."

Words From the Word

Finally, beloved, whatever is true, whatever is honorable, whatever is just, whatever is pure, whatever is pleasing, whatever is commendable, if there is any excellence and if there is anything worthy of praise, think about these things.

–Philippians 4:8

Other Voices

There's no beauty like the beauty of the soul.

–North Carolina proverb

People are like stained glass windows—the true beauty can be seen only from within.

–Elisabeth Kubler-Ross

I believe that children are our future. Teach them well and let them lead the way. Show them all the beauty they possess inside.

–Whitney Houston

[External] beauty fades...dumb is forever.

–Judge Judy

Bottom Line

An attractive appearance is a fine gift—that you receive. Becoming a beautiful person on the inside is an even greater gift—that you *give* to others simply by being who you are—and is based on becoming a truly loving person.

FOUR

Seeing Things in Perspective

Then Jesus said to him, "What do you want me to do for you?" The blind man said to him, "My Teacher, let me see again."

–*Mark 10:51*

If you ever want your immediate future ruined, try having emergency eye surgery. It's really nasty—not so much the actual surgery, because you're off in Whatever Land while that's going on. But for quite some time afterward, you're not allowed to do things you enjoy doing—like playing racquetball. I love the game, and after my surgery, I wasn't allowed to play for several months. It bothered the heck out of me.

I had gone to the eye doctor and he told me that I had a detached retina in my right eye. If it's not caught and corrected in time, you go practically blind in the eye. An eye surgeon operated on mine the very next morning. "You don't want to wait with something like this," he said.

Problem was, that morning I was supposed to be on the racquetball court. Instead, I was lying on an operating table at Christ Hospital having my retina reattached. Believe me, that's not nearly as much fun as slamming a kill shot into the corner of the court or driving your opponent nuts with a perfect lob serve to his backhand.

Well, the surgery was successful, and eventually I regained full vision in that eye. But it took weeks to get my stroke back, and I lost quite a few games during that time.

Maybe you're thinking, "*You idiot!* You had your eyesight saved, and you're whining about missing a few games of racquetball?"

At least I hope you're thinking that.

And, actually, that wasn't my real reaction to the surgery. I was trying to provide an example of looking at things very much out of perspective. Sure, I missed racquetball, but I was mainly grateful to God and Dr. Kranias. I missed some games, but when I got back on the court, I knew I was going to be able to see the ball for many games to come. It was an awfully good trade.

Seeing the events of life out of perspective is like staring into a carnival mirror that makes you look as though you've gained or lost ninety pounds or makes your face appear to be 85 percent nose. Instead of exaggerating or minimizing body features, however, seeing things out of perspective makes events in our lives seem much less or much more important than they really are—or much better or much worse than they really are.

Example: You set the VCR to tape the season finale of *The Dysfunctional Lives of Meebles Crossing* because you have a meeting and you'll miss the show when it airs. According to previews, in this episode Lorinda will finally tell Brett what really happened when the SWAT team was mistakenly sent to the tanning salon during a hurricane while Nelle was there to meet Ashford to discuss the future of their relationship, which had been threatened by his boyhood promise to Aunt Melba to join the circus.

The next day you turn on the TV, rewind the tape, hit the play button, and Senator Windmeister is vigorously disagreeing with Senator Laimskeem's proposal to put a federal tax on goldfish. *NO!* Somehow you mistakenly taped C-SPAN!

You, of course, would simply think, "Oh, well...I can ask somebody what happened. It's just a TV show."

But some people would throw a fit. "Stupid, stupid VCR! I missed the *season finale!*" They might even add certain interjections. They might go around in a funk for the rest of the day or more.

An example from the other side: Your World Cultures teacher calls you aside after class one day and informs you that your research paper was not all that great, along with the last couple of tests, and that you're on the bubble for passing, and you'll need a very good grade on the final.

You, of course, would be very concerned. You would

ask your teacher what minimum grade on the final will it take to pass; what much better grade will it take to bring your average up to a C; and is it possible, perhaps with an extra credit project, to bring it up to a B-minus. Armed with this information, you would sign up for study sessions after school, pull the plug on your television viewing, and put a temporary brake on your social life.

But some people would tell themselves, "Okay, I guess I have to study more, but it's no problem because the final is still three weeks away."

What a fantastic skill it would be always to know exactly how important something is *when it happens!* We can't control all of the things that happen in our lives, but we can choose our attitude toward them. That includes placing them on a scale that ranks importance or significance.

Historians are always telling us to learn from the past, which is excellent advice. The past in this case, however, is not things like the War of 1812. The past here is specifically *your* past. A simple exercise can help. List some past events in your life that fall under one of the following two categories.

1. *Good things or fun things that weren't as great as they seemed at the time, or which haven't had a lasting impact.*

Take party invitations, for example. You got invited to an event with *the* group. Social success! Reputation! For a while, something like that can feel like it's the best thing that ever happened to you. But how permanent has that status been? Was that party or event really a determining factor in your life? If it happened several years ago, where are the people in the group now? How important are they in your life?

Concerts and vacations and computer games and just-released CDs from the currently hottest artists can easily fall into this category also. There's nothing wrong with them, nothing wrong with thoroughly enjoying them, but they hardly qualify as biggies when it comes to fulfillment in life. When we give them higher status than they deserve, genuinely important things can get neglected.

Now see if you can detect a pattern on the things that fall into this category. Are they mostly social events? Opportunities to perform or be noticed? Stuff to buy, such as clothes and jewelry? Entertainment items?

If you see a pattern, it can help you judge similar things more accurately when they seem like "must have" items at the time and spare you some frustration.

2. Disappointments or setbacks that haven't turned out to be nearly as bad as they felt at the time.

Reverse the party invitation situation. This time you were (perhaps once again) excluded, or for some reason you weren't able to go or weren't allowed to go, even though "everybody" was going to be there. How fatal has that loss been to your social life? Do you lie awake at night, mourning over that missed golden episode of perfect fun?

Several years ago, I was talking (after a game of racquetball, actually) with a student who mentioned being out of the social loop as far as the cool people (or so he thought at the time) and popular girls were concerned. He was a little shy, but another reason is that he wouldn't drink or do some of the other on-the-edge activities that those people were doing. It wasn't exactly tearing him apart, but he would have liked to have had a more active social life, and he was not particularly hopeful about finding a really attractive girl who would like him.

Two years ago I did one of the Scripture readings at his wedding. He and his truly beautiful bride are extremely happy. At the reception, I reminded him of our conversation several years before and playfully asked him whether he still missed the parties he hadn't been invited to.

"What parties?" he grinned.

It reminded me a bit of the story line in Garth Brooks' song, "Unanswered Prayers." The girl he longed for, whose attention he literally prayed for, didn't return his attention. But when he meets that girl years later and compares her to his wife, he's extremely grateful that it turned out that way.

Once again, see whether you can detect a pattern in the events that fall into this category. Were the "losses" that turned out to be not much of a loss at all mostly social events? Relationship hopes? Employment opportunities?

* * *

I'm not saying that if you have your mind on straight, nothing will ever hurt very much at the time—just spray a little Perspective Painkiller on the disappointment, and everything will feel just fine. And I'm not suggesting that you distrust or tone down your enjoyment of positive things simply because they're not likely to be grounds for permanent good fortune and happiness.

Seeing things in perspective is not walking through life numb to both joy and sorrow. If somebody says they'll go out with you, enjoy the rush, enjoy the gift. If somebody breaks up with you, don't pretend it doesn't matter and doesn't hurt. That's not seeing things in perspective; that's denial. Seeing things in perspective simply means comparing their value, whether positive or negative, with the value of other things in your life.

If someone says they'll go out with you, or if you make the team or the cast of the play, perspective helps you realize that you still have other relationships and other obligations that need care and attention. It would be a mistake to let the rush of success blind you to them.

When something bad or sad happens, usually the last thing you want to hear is "It's not the end of the world," because it may feel that way for a while. And one "world" may indeed have come to an end, as when a relationship ends. But if that happens, or if you get cut from the team or the cast, perspective helps you realize (even through the pain) that "what's now is not forever." Perspective helps you see that this "world" is not you and your entire life, no matter how much the loss hurts at the time.

Something you might call "perspective plus" takes this a step further and leads you to ask, "What can I learn from this?" or "How can I turn this setback into an advantage of some kind?" Again, that's not denying the hurt or the disappointment. It's a matter of not letting the hurt and disappointment become the whole experience.

Spraining an ankle and being sidelined from a sport isn't exactly a lucky break. But it does free up a good bit of time for a while. "Perspective plus" asks, "How can I use the extra time to get ahead or do a better job in some other area?" Being sidelined from the racquetball court for a while after eye surgery freed up a lot of time to get ahead on writing deadlines.

Putting things in perspective can work forward as well as backward. It can help us plan things to do, as well as help us respond to things that happen. When I would ask my students what was really important to them, their lists were really very similar. At the top were parents and family, friends, health, education and good grades, sports, goals for the future, and God. Your list would probably include many of those same things.

A "perspective check" can help us examine our lives and see whether the things we list as important are really being given time enough to match their importance. Life does get busy and crowded with details that have to be taken care of. Showering and putting on clean clothes are not likely to make anybody's "Most Important to Me" list, but we certainly don't want to neglect doing them. At the same time, it's easy to get so caught up in attending to the details of the day that we give too little time to the things that we ourselves say matter most— God and family, for example.

The greatest help toward seeing things as they really are and responding accordingly is faith. Pray over what delights you. Pray over what saddens you. It doesn't have to be a fancy prayer. "Lord, please help me to see this correctly and respond in the way you want" works just fine.

Words From the Word

I know what it is to have little, and I know what it is to have plenty. In any and all circumstances I have learned the secret of being well-fed and of going hungry, of having plenty and of being in need. I can do all things through him who strengthens me.

—Philippians 4:12–13

I want you to know, beloved, that what has happened to me has actually helped to spread the gospel, so that it has become known throughout the whole imperial guard and to everyone else that my imprisonment is for Christ.

—Philippians 1:12–13

Other Voices

Do not lose your inward peace for anything whatsoever, even if your whole world seems upset.

—Saint Francis de Sales

To a brave person, good and bad luck are like his right and left hand. He uses both.

–Saint Catherine of Siena

Bottom Line

Seeing things in perspective is not walking through life numb to both joy and sorrow. Seeing things in perspective simply means comparing their value, whether positive or negative, with the value of other things in your life.

FIVE

Manners Matter

Let your speech always be gracious, seasoned with salt, so that you may know how to answer everyone.

–Colossians 4:6

Remember the scene in *Titanic* in which Jack Dawson attends an elaborate dinner to which he's been invited by Rose's parents. They really don't like Jack, but after all, he did save their daughter's life.

Fortunately, Jack doesn't have to show up in scruffs—the only kind of clothes he owns—thanks to "the unsinkable" Molly Brown who outfits him in total gentlemanly elegance. And he acts accordingly. He approaches Rose with slow-paced dignity, gives her a courtly bow, gently kisses her hand, offers her his arm, and escorts her to dinner. When we watch this scene, we think: *That's class...that's cool.*

What if Jack had shown up dressed in the same killer

clothes but had slouched up to Rose with his mouth working on a wad of gum, kept his hands in his pockets, shrugged his shoulders and said, "Hey, girl." Not quite the same scene, is it?

Our appreciation of Jack Dawson's style shows we realize that there is a place for good manners, that social cluelessness is not funny, and that crude does not equal cool.

What exactly *are* good manners? Your mom or grandma would probably tell you they're about saying "please" and "thank you." A dictionary will run you through slight variations of "polite customs." In the end, though, it comes down to this: good manners are ways of showing *respect* for people and for occasions or situations that deserve special behavior. This is what Jack Dawson is doing in the scene from *Titanic*. *He's showing respect for Rose*—not because she's wealthy but because she's Rose—and for the occasion, a formal dinner.

Bad manners? It's probably accurate enough to define deliberate bad manners as ways of showing *disrespect* for people and occasions.

That's more serious than simple social cluelessness because it gets us into the arena of moral right and wrong. It's not *morally wrong* to use the wrong piece of silverware at an elegant banquet, or even to burp in public just because you're dumb enough to think crude behavior is hilarious. But bad manners that deliberately show disrespect for others are more than social cluelessness—they're *wrong*.

Reasons for using good manners and being courteous are both obvious and plentiful. They range from the practical to the genuinely spiritual. Let's look at a few.

Courtesy and good manners are simple and effective ways to literally carry out the command of Jesus to respect and love other people. Whether you hold the door for someone, say please and thank you, or pick up an item that someone has dropped, your action says that you value the other person, that he or she is worthwhile and important—a *person*, not just a piece of furniture in your life.

Courtesy and good manners, in other words, are literally a type of love. Not the kind that leads to warm, dreamy coziness, marriage, and parenthood, but actual love nevertheless.

So if, at the end of the day, you're wondering whether or not you loved others, whether or not you did what Jesus would have done, one way to check is to look at the manners you displayed during the day. If you were courteous when the occasion called for courtesy, put a mental checkmark in the "loved others" column. Courtesy isn't the whole picture of loving others, but it's a definite part of it.

"Courtesy is like oil on troubled waters," says a Kansas proverb, and from New York comes the saying, "Courtesy is one of the best peacemakers." These undoubtedly refer to patching up a misunderstanding or a quarrel with someone, but it goes beyond that.

A little courtesy can do a lot to comfort someone who's having a troubled, unpeaceful day for reasons that have nothing to do with you. Example: Somebody drops his or her books coming out of a classroom after having failed a physics test, and you pick them up. You hear, "Thanks," and you respond, "You're welcome," in a pleasant voice. That doesn't raise the grade to 95 percent but it sprays a decent dose of emotional salve on the 67 percent.

Simply put, good manners and genuine courtesy can be religious gestures. They do not appear as religious as heartily singing "How Great Thou Art" at the end of a worship service, but religion doesn't end with the closing hymn. If it did, we'd have to change the name from "religion" to "interesting spiritual hobby." Religious acts aren't out of bounds once we walk out of church.

Personal reward should not be the principal reason for using good manners and showing courtesy, but there's nothing wrong with enjoying the benefits of doing so. Far more often than not, winners in life are likely to be courteous people.

The person who firmly shakes the manager's hand, looks her in the eye, and says "Thank you for your time" at a job interview has a huge edge in getting the position over someone who glances around the room and says, "Izzat all?"

"It takes fifteen seconds to make a first impression, and it could take the rest of your life to undo it if it is a negative one," stated an article in a business magazine.

Unfortunately, some people see good manners and courtesy as signs of weakness, dependence, and even immaturity (although it's really the opposite of the latter).

That image is about as accurate as the idea that the Sun revolves around the Earth.

Here's proof: Babies have the worst manners of all. Babies never say please or thank you or excuse me. They think only of their own needs and constantly insist on those needs being met. They never introduce themselves politely, and they routinely interrupt conversations. They often ignore people around them and pay no attention to what is said to them. They knock things over and never apologize or help pick up the items. They often make crude sounds in public.

That's classic *infant behavior.*

Consequently, *the same behavior from someone who is no longer an actual infant* does not exactly indicate a strong, independent person who understands what life in the real world is all about.

Extending courtesy to adults is sometimes considered sucking up. Of course, it *could* be, but it isn't always or even usually, and it shouldn't be judged as such.

One year, a new kid came to the school where I taught. After his first class with me, he came to me in the hall, extended his hand, and said, "It was good to meet you. I enjoyed the class."

Are you picturing a scrawny, sucking-up geek trying to grease his way into an A? No. He was about 6'2", a solid 200 or so pounds, and he did not always make a career of becoming every teacher's model student. But he knew how to be a gentleman. He knew how to pour a little courteous oil on the sometimes-choppy waters of a school day.

Some people see bad manners and a lack of courtesy as signs of strength, independence, coolness, and even humor. This image gets a strong boost in media that portray rude and crude as funny.

But where exactly is the *strength* in letting the door slam behind us instead of holding it open for the person following? Where's the *power* or *personal worth* in not apologizing after we've hurt someone, even if it was unintentional?

Never saying thanks for things received—that's independence? Maybe people who seldom thank others should really *prove* their independence by *never needing or accepting anything* from anyone! For example, if they're too independent to say thanks for a meal someone cooked for them, maybe they should be independent enough to cook their own meals…using food they've brought home after buying it themselves—with their own money, of course.

Ignoring other people, including those who have worked hard on someone's behalf…not responding to or even acknowledging a greeting—those behaviors are cool? About as cool as going on a date without having bathed or changed clothes for a week or so.

Where exactly is the humor in making someone feel anywhere from unappreciated to rejected? Where's the amusement in making someone feel like a piece of lint on the carpet instead of like a person in the room?

True, what makes up "good manners" sometimes depends on the occasion. If a guy gives a girl a courtly bow and a princely kiss on her hand as they meet at Wendy's and then offers his arm to escort her to the

"Order Here" station…well, let's just say it's not quite necessary or expected in that setting.

Saying "sorry" and/or "excuse me" if you happen to bump into somebody on the bus is necessary and expected behavior. Saying the same things (and meaning them) if you happen to bump into somebody as you're going up for a rebound is a sign you should be playing chess instead of basketball.

Jesus calls us to love one another and treat others as we would want to be treated. Good manners and courtesy are a part of both.

Words From the Word

But now you must get rid of all such things—anger, wrath, malice, slander, and abusive language from your mouth.

–Colossians 3:8

A gentle tongue is a tree of life.

–Proverbs 15:4

Other Voices

Bad manners are a species of bad morals.

–Kansas proverb

There is nothing that costs so little nor goes so far as courtesy.

–Nebraska proverb

Bottom Line

There are many reasons for acting with courtesy and good manners. The most important is that it is a way of showing others the respect and love that Jesus calls us to give them.

SIX

The Blame Game

Do not be reckless in your speech, / or sluggish and remiss in your deeds.

—Sirach 4:29

Teaching taught me a lot of things I never would have suspected otherwise.

For example, students do not lose papers that teachers give them. The papers get lost all by themselves. Some papers are so scatterbrained that they can't keep themselves inside a binder or a book bag for more than a day.

If a notice sent home to parents doesn't get signed and returned, the parents are at fault, as proven by the ironclad testimony, "They didn't sign it." The student is not involved in the process at all.

When students do poorly on a test, they do so in spite of having studied for hours. Studying for hours, therefore, is obviously the wrong approach to doing well. Why repeat a technique that just isn't working?

Okay, I'm picking on some students when obviously it's not only students who sometimes avoid responsibility. I've avoided responsibility myself a few times here and there—but that was only because I was influenced by the hippies during my college days, and also because my wife has occasionally put up with it, which she never should have done.

Taking responsibility for our actions when we mess up, fail, or just don't get the job done is not fun, and even more so when other people know about it and aren't happy. Let's say I mess up, and therefore my wife isn't happy or my boss isn't happy or my colleagues aren't happy—and sometimes I suspect that God isn't delighted, either. That doesn't feel good. It can be positively painful.

We've been told probably way too often that when we're in pain, we should reach for the first available painkiller. In this case, the painkiller is called Blame. "I couldn't help it because…" "It wasn't my fault because…" I didn't have any choice because…" "But…" Does this work? Yes and no. Actually, it's more like *maybe* and no.

"Maybe," because the people who are upset *may* believe that I was indeed in the grip of forces beyond my control and therefore not hold me accountable. (And then again, they may *not* believe it even though they don't tell me that.)

"No" because, first of all, *I* know that I'm avoiding responsibility and that takes away a chunk of my self-respect. Second, in most cases I still have to do what I didn't get done or make up for what I did wrong.

Can something outside yourself ever cause a bad break or keep you from accomplishing a task or achieving a goal? Of course. However, that's not the case nearly as often as we'd like to think it is. We are, or could be, far more in control of our lives than we might be comfortable with. It's easier and less demanding to be a passenger on our ship than to be the captain in command of it and responsible for how it performs and where it goes.

Let's pretend that there's a product called Soothe-All and that you have a sprained wrist. Soothe-All works pretty well. It takes away a lot of the pain—as long as you keep using it. But there's a catch. As long as you keep using it, it prevents the wrist from getting healing treatment.

Blame is a lot like that. It seems to reduce the pain of having failed or made a mistake. But when you use it, it keeps you from learning from the mistake and sets you up to make the same mistake, or a similar one, again.

Blaming (and, usually, the whining that goes along with it) has been going on for a *really* long time. Take the Genesis 3:1–16 story. The world's first people get busted for eating the forbidden fruit. God confronts Adam about it. Adam doesn't deny it...but is it his *fault?*

Of course not! Who's *really* to blame? Eve...*and God!* "The woman gave me the fruit from the tree, so I ate it. What else could I do—I have to live with her! And incidentally, *you* put her here. If you hadn't put her here, this never would have happened." (Paraphrase of Genesis 3:12.)

Eve doesn't deny her fruit snack either, but is it *her fault?* Of course not! That rotten old *serpent* is responsible. "The serpent tricked me. I got spiritually mugged—I'm a *victim!*" (Paraphrase of Genesis 3:13.)

We learn to blame early in life. When we were young, we didn't know we were supposed to (or not to). Somebody told us to do it. Somebody made us do it. Somebody did it first. It just happened, and we didn't even realize we were doing it. And on and on and on.

But we're supposed to grow out of that. When we don't, blaming—and therefore excusing ourselves—can become practically a lifestyle. Call it Constant Blame/Excusing Syndrome. It has some really undesirable consequences.

1. *It becomes an automatic reaction to any mistake or fault.* There's nothing wrong with some automatic reactions. You feel a sneeze coming on, and you reach for a handkerchief. A bus is headed directly toward your body, and you politely step out of the way. Someone offers you a joint, and you suggest where he or she can put it. Those and many more automatic reactions are good. Automatically blaming and excusing is not.

Unfortunately, we can get really good at it. Example:

"Bill, you don't have your assignment...again."

"I couldn't do it. My book was at school."

"You need to check your assignment list at the end of the day and make sure you have what you need."

"I was going to, but Jason kept asking me questions about stuff, and that took my mind off of it, and by then I was late for my ride."

"There were only three questions. You could have called somebody and gotten them and still done the assignment based on what we talked about in class."

"I tried to call Angela, but she wasn't home."

"That's the only person you could have called?"

"My mom was on the phone after that."

And so on...and on. The words vary from one situation to another and from one age level to the next, but the scenario is the same.

If you do it often enough, this kind of response begins to shape the way you see and feel about yourself. Instead of picturing yourself as capable and in charge of your life, you begin to see yourself as a victim. From there, it's easy to begin talking and acting like a victim all the time.

2. *You stop growing.* "We learn by doing," the educator Thomas Dewey said, and he might have reasonably added, "including making mistakes." That's part of life. You look at what you did wrong, figure out how and why, decide to do it differently the next time, and go on from there. That's growth. That's healthy.

The Blame/Excuse Syndrome keeps it from happening. When you blame something or somebody else for your mistakes or failures, you give up the power to change or improve your life. Since some *other* thing is *causing* your problems, all you can do is wait for it to stop—or for something stronger to start preventing your problems. In either case, it's all outside of you. You're a piece on the chessboard of life, not a player.

A lifestyle of habitual blaming leads to "victimhood." I have ADHD, so don't expect me to succeed in school because I can never learn to concentrate. My father left us, so don't expect me to learn how to act like a man. My mother is an alcoholic, so don't expect me to be able to control my drinking. I'm a minority, so I'm automatically oppressed; don't expect me to try hard because it won't do any good anyway. I'm white, so I won't get hired because most places need to hire minorities. I'm kind of plain looking and therefore nobody will ever really like me, so don't expect me to act likable. I was born with a bad temper, so don't expect me to behave peacefully. I'm shy, so don't expect me to make friends. My older brother is in jail, so don't expect me to keep the law.

In this final stage, blaming is more than an automatic response. It's an attitude you carry around all the time. It's the *state of mind you start from*. That's fatal. Your body is still pumping blood, but your motivation, determination, and effort are close to dead.

3. *It sustains a false "perfect verses zero" mentality.* This mentality says that if I make a mistake, any mistake, I'm substandard, not worth much. That's ridiculous, of course, but unfortunately kind of common.

Nobody likes to feel substandard, so once again the attempted painkiller—"But it wasn't my fault because I couldn't help it, so it's *not really a mistake*"—comes in to rescue me and attempts to restore my self-esteem.

That puts an enormous burden on daily life. If I feel I

have to be mistake-free to be okay (or okay in someone else's eyes), then I have to find something or someone to blame every time I don't perform perfectly...or at least every time someone else sees me not performing perfectly. It also backfires. Instead of coming across as someone who almost never makes a real mistake, I come across as an excuse factory and a whiner.

* * *

Blaming and excusing versus taking responsibility isn't limited to success or failure in school, athletics, or a career. It's a big factor in our life of faith.

God did not create us to be Ping-Pong balls. Each of us was created by God to become a fully alive, unique human being and a unique reflection of God. A lifestyle of blaming and excusing reduces us to much less than the picture God had in mind of who we could be.

If we habitually blame someone or something else for things like missing assignments or not getting the job done at home or at work, it becomes easy to excuse ourselves for doing things that are genuinely morally wrong. At the start, "I couldn't help it" or "That's just the way I am" seems to excuse us for missing an English assignment, being late for work, or not taking out the trash. Then it begins to excuse us for hurting people's feelings, being selfish and greedy, abusing alcohol or other drugs, engaging in violent behavior—almost anything.

Changing a habit or even a slight trend of blaming and excusing doesn't happen easily or overnight. Like any negative habit, it takes awhile to get rid of it and replace it with a positive habit—in this case, of taking full responsibility for everything you should be responsible for. And it's, well, kind of scary at first.

It starts with learning and recognizing what you really can and cannot control. You can't control what you were born with or where, and you can't control things that happen to you that you could not possibly have foreseen.

But you *can* control how you respond to those things. You can control what you do with them and how you deal with them. You can control your attitude. That's actually very freeing, as well as initially scary.

And it's freeing to admit that frequently you still crowd the ball.

I've taught over two hundred of my students to play racquetball. One of the most common initial mistakes is to get too close to the ball. You can't hit it very well when it's right in front of you. A soccer ball off your chest, yes. A racquetball right in front of your chest, no.

"Don't crowd the ball," I would say over and over. And I'd be hopeful about that person's future on the court when I would hear, "Yeah, I know—I did it again. I'll remember next time."

But if someone had repeatedly said, "I *didn't* crowd the ball—the ball just got too close to me and I couldn't do anything about it," I would have worried about that person's future in racquetball—and in life.

Words From the Word

The lazy person says [as an excuse for doing nothing], "There is a lion in the road! There is a lion in the streets!"

–Proverbs 26:13

Other Voices

In terms of personal happiness, you *cannot* be peaceful while at the same time blaming others. Blaming makes you feel powerless over your own life because your happiness is contingent on the actions and behavior of others, which you can't control. When you stop blaming, you regain your sense of personal power.

–Richard Carlson

It has long since come to my attention that people of accomplishment rarely sat back and let things happen to them. They went out and happened to things.

–Elinor Smith

Bottom Line

When we habitually blame something or somebody else for our mistakes or failures, we give up the power to change or improve our lives. We even close ourselves off to accepting God's help to change or improve our lives.

God did not create us to be Ping-Pong balls. God created us to mature into a reflection of God's goodness and glory.

SEVEN

Handling Stress on the Road to Success

Moreover, it is God's gift that all should eat and
drink and take pleasure in all their toil.

–*Ecclesiastes 3:13*

Accoding to an old saying, a diamond is a piece of
coal that did well under pressure. You remember
from earth science that coal and diamonds are basically
carbon. Enormous pressure slowly turns a common carbon, coal, into a rare carbon, a diamond. (Don't put a
lump of coal under a heavy object and expect to get rich.
You'll never live to see the result.)

Enormous pressure is wonderful for a piece of coal
on its way to a jewelry case. But what about people?
Young people report feeling tremendous pressure to succeed. How much pressure is too much—and just what is
success, anyway?

High-school students often cite getting good grades and being accepted into a good college as their two biggest pressures. College students cite getting good grades and then securing a good job in a desirable career.

This pressure begins with the lifestyle that our society looks up to and views as the ideal. Unfortunately, the salary you earn, the car you drive, and the type of house and neighborhood in which you live often define it. A poet who lives in a third-floor apartment doesn't receive much prestige; an account executive living in a new four-bedroom home in suburban sprawl does.

Parents may reinforce that view. This doesn't mean they're bad parents. They want the best for their children as they see it. Sometimes, even without actually saying so, they tend to measure success in terms of career and the figures that follow the dollar sign on a paycheck.

Schools are usually under pressure to improve their programs, which often translates into making them more demanding. The pressure gets passed on to teachers and then to students.

Working very hard toward academic and career success is certainly not evil or unhealthy. Neither is feeling some pressure to get there. What isn't good is pressure that takes too heavy a toll, demands too high a price, or creates a narrow, warped, or just plain wrong view of life and oneself.

IAMGS is one of the latter. Don't try to pronounce it; the human mouth and tongue are not designed to bend in that direction. IAMGS stands for "I Am My Grades Syndrome."

Unless Mom or Dad owns the corporation, grades are usually the biggest initial factor on the Great American Road to Successful Adult life. Even before kids begin to think about success or career, they pick up the idea that "good kids" get good grades. Parents can reinforce this idea without meaning to when a child brings home a "good" test paper. They say, "I'm so proud of you" (which is fine) and then, perhaps, "You're such a good boy/girl"—which is a mistake to say right at that particular time. The conclusion is: good grades = good kid.

So for at least a dozen years, often far more than that, it may seem logical to answer such questions as "Am I worthwhile?" and "How good a person am I?" in terms of grades—even if deep inside you don't agree with that method of judging.

Sometimes this causes a frustration or even a little anger. If you're getting straight As or close to it, people expect you to continue doing so pretty much without exception. Maybe you are the only one who knows the immense effort it takes to pull off this academic class act, and you wish the occasional B would not seem a relative failure.

Or perhaps for you, a B- is a great victory that also requires immense effort. But you sense that the results of this effort still don't look as good as an A. At the same time, deep inside you feel you're just as good a *person* as the classmates who have season tickets to the honor roll or the dean's list.

So here comes an important truth: *You are not your*

grades. They're only one part of your makeup as a teen or young adult.

If your grades are as good as you can make them, whatever that may be, pin a mental medal on yourself and thank God for the academic gifts you've been given. If your grades are a lot lower *than they could be*, you're still a wonderful, lovable, spectacularly worthwhile child of God. However, you may be closing some doors to your future that, when the future arrives, you'll wish hadn't been closed. Yes, you can always start over, but seldom under the same circumstances or with the same opportunities.

Similar to IAMGS is IAMCS: "I Am My Career Syndrome." This rates occupations according to high, medium, or lower salary and image in terms of worth and honor. "High" means more respectable and more honorable than any that are "lower."

That's bad enough, but it goes on to rate the person and his or her worth based on one's job. If you're the executive vice president in charge of marketing research for Transco-Omnicom-Multistuff International, you're a valuable, successful human being. If you're on their maintenance staff, well, it's a shame you didn't make more of yourself.

That's...well, an old-fashioned and relatively polite term is hogwash.

Now I need to clarify something. I'm not downplaying the value of working hard to become executive vice president—or the talent and effort it takes to get there. A lofty career goal is not evil, and this is not a call to downshift effort from high gear in favor of simply vegging out in a low-key, pressure-free existence. The hippies tried that in the sixties, and it was not exactly a stunning success. This is simply an effort to put things in balance.

It would be helpful to have a reliable stress meter that would accurately determine each person's level of stress. Tape a few electrodes onto your skin, flip the switch, and check the screen, which would say, "Too Much Stress—Relax Already!" or "Too Little Stress—Get Your Butt Moving!" or "Just Right—Proceed As You Are." Alas (love that word; seldom get a chance to use it), there is no such machine.

But there are some signs that indicate either you are genuinely under too much pressure and it's creating an unhealthy situation or that your pressure is not necessarily unreasonable, but you need to handle it better.

- Dishonesty in the form of cheating on tests or exams, downloading packaged reports and term papers, and so on. It's tempting to rationalize this behavior as okay because the goal (a successful career) is good. (It's also worth noting, that this same behavior can likewise be a sign of plain old laziness.)
- Taking stimulants such as caffeine pills or even heavier uppers. A few cups of coffee or tea are part of most students' academic life. But if academic survival is dependent on chemical stimulation, something needs repair.
- Excessive weekend partying and binge drinking

in order to come down Stress Mountain. "Everybody needs to unwind." Absolutely. But not by being unable to remember parts of Saturday and/or Sunday. Not by beginning Monday in a mental fog.

- General unhappiness and depression. It's one thing to wish you were on spring break or summer vacation. It's another to wake up every day feeling you'll never get out from under the huge load you're carrying, and wondering if there's any meaning to it all. (Don't confuse the latter with the occasional, "What do we have to know *this* for?" Students have been thinking that since the time of Socrates.)
- Slacking—just getting by in spite of proven ability.
- Being extremely busy and worn out all the time. Sometimes excessive pressure is self-created, simply by taking on too many activities. More often than not, they're all good. There are just too many of them.

How do you determine whether you're genuinely under too much pressure from too many obligations, or you're just not handling pressure well?

It often translates into how you handle time. Keep an exact log of where your time goes for a week or two. I know, this sounds like adding still another thing to do into your already busy life, but it's helpful, often eye opening, and sometimes positively shocking. It'll work only if you're brutally honest with yourself, and only if you track a truly typical time period. So don't pick the week before exams or the three or four days spent cranking out a research paper that was assigned six weeks ago.

If you discover that you've averaged four or five hours of sleep per night and done almost nothing but study and work during the day—and there's no relief in sight until you finish finals or graduate—making some changes is in order.

Get an opinion from someone who is qualified and willing to tell you the truth (not someone who is almost guaranteed, no matter what, to say, "I don't know how you take all that pressure, life is kickin' you in the butt, it ain't fair, etc.")

This *could* be a totally honest friend, classmate, or roommate. It's more likely to be someone who can judge from a distance and from experience, such as a school counselor or academic advisor. Don't forget to bring your brutally honest time log when you see him or her.

"You'll know you're a success when…" I have no idea how to complete that sentence. Well, that's not true. I don't know how to choose *the* best way out of all the ways that I think would be valid.

Two of the finest young men I know graduated from college a couple years ago. One of them majored in information systems with a minor in management. He stepped into a sixty-thousand-dollar-a-year job…that's the *starting* salary. The corporation that hired him made the down payment on a home as a signing bonus and will pay for his further education. A six-figure salary is definitely in his future, and probably not too far away.

The other applied to Jesuit Volunteers International and committed to two years of volunteer service in Tanzania. For two years, he taught, ministered, and served people in a culture immensely different from his own. His "salary" was simply knowing that he had helped. When he returned to the States, he took a job teaching high-school math. A six-figure salary is about as likely as a vacation on the moon.

Which one is a success? It depends on the vision, the definition, the model, which sociologists like to call a "paradigm." A business or commercial paradigm would point to the first young man as beginning to claim, work for, and live what has sometimes been called "The American Dream." A religious paradigm would probably point to the second young man as embracing the Gospel value of Christian service.

I consider each of them a roaring success.

Real success in life has very little to do with lifestyle. Real success in life lies in becoming a saint. As the wise monk Thomas Merton pointed out in *Seeds of Contemplation,* "For me to be a saint means to be myself." Sanctity for each of us is being and becoming the person God created us to be, and doing the best job we can of it.

I see both of these young men becoming their true selves in what they're doing. And the world needs each of them.

We need Christians who give their life directly to the

service of others. We also need Christians to be key players in the competitive business world. Some people might
say we need committed, uncompromising, rock-solidly
ethical Christians there more than in most places.

Somewhere, in some way, the world needs *you* to be
a success yourself, to be your own unique saint—a diamond that did well under pressure.

Words From the Word

[Jesus] said to them, "Come away to a deserted
place all by yourselves and rest a while." For many
had been coming and going, and they had no lei-
sure even to eat.

–*Mark 6:31*

For everything there is a season, and a time for
every matter under heaven.

–*Ecclesiastes 3:1*

Other Voices

There are no secrets to success. It is the result of
preparation, hard work, and learning from failure.

–*General Colin L. Powell*

He has achieved success who has lived well,
laughed often, and loved much.

–*Bessie Anderson*

Bottom Line

Success amounts to becoming the person you were created to be, whoever that is and whatever he/she has been called to do—and managing the legitimate stress it takes to get there.

EIGHT

The Race Is On...
But What's the Prize?

Do you not know that in a race the runners all
compete, but only one receives the prize? Run in
such a way that you may win it.

–1 Corinthians 9:24

I was once thinking about my introduction to the next
grammar unit on subordinate clauses and complex
sentences. Actually, I had three possibilities in mind,
and I wasn't sure which one to go with. See what you
think.

1. "Okay, students, these next several days will determine whether you're real English students or just poor,
inferior imitations. I've put each of you on a team of
five. Your job is to toughen up both yourselves and your
teammates. Work, push, drive, and whip yourselves and

your teammates into top grammatical condition. Devour every practice sheet you can find.

"The teams will then compete in the final exam. One team will win the glory and the prize—a passing grade for the quarter. The others will fail. That's just what life is: *competition!* The winner takes the prize, and the others just kind of slide off the road of life into a ditch and get forgotten with nothing to show for their efforts.

"Yes, some teams have more natural talent than others. That makes it all the more glorious when a team of former grammatical zeroes upsets a naturally talented team. That's the way life is, too."

2. "Okay, students, these next several days will be an adventure in cooperating with one another in order to help each of you grow. I've divided the class into cooperative learning groups. Each group is composed of people with differing gifts and talents. Your job is to recognize and use these different gifts and talents to achieve the group goal: an understanding of subordinate clauses and complex sentences.

"You are competing not so much with other groups but with your own group's best self. Grades will be assigned on each group's average at the end of the unit, with bonus points awarded to groups that have shown outstanding cooperation and mutual reinforcement. Fifteen bonus points will be awarded to the group with the best team hug."

3. "Okay, kids, I've divided you into groups, and I want

you to spend your time studying the unit on subordinate clauses and complex sentences. Help one another as much as you can, and try to learn as much as you can, but I don't want you to feel pressured. That's not good for you.

"There will be kind of an evaluation when you're finished, but it's not like a test or anything, so no pressure, okay? If, at the end, you still don't know a subordinate clause from a grapefruit, I have some beautifully embossed certificates for Outstanding Page-Turning."

Actually, I didn't use any of those three approaches in teaching grammar. I used the simple, effective method of *threat:* Pass or you'll have to attend remedial classes after school, during which I will sing Old English folk ballads in my unique style of three notes off-key.

* * *

Competition...is it good or bad? Does God approve of it? Does God recommend it? It's not a simple question, and you won't find any simple agreement. The examples above illustrate three different views.

1. *Yes.* Competition drives people toward achievement. Intense competition molds winners. God wants people to be winners in life.
2. *Sort of.* Competition with one's own best self is the best type, as long as the person is supported by cooperation from many other people. God wants people to grow.
3. *No!* People should feel good about themselves without any reference to achievement—and measuring

achievement is unfair. It's socially biased against people who don't achieve. God wants people to feel how good they are no matter what.

Where are you on the idea of competition? You'll probably say, "It depends." Sometimes that's an avoidance answer, but in this case it's probably a common-sense reaction.

First of all, it depends on the arena. Some arenas of life are competitive by nature. Sports obviously come to mind. Of course when six-year-olds are playing T-ball, the final score is no big deal and actually no deal at all. It doesn't matter much to the players because they all get taken out for burgers or ice cream afterwards, and that's the main event for them anyway. But later in life, the score matters. If a high-school player or coach said, "It doesn't matter" when asked about the prospect of winning the City title, you'd wonder why they were even part of the team.

We also compete academically. Everybody wants a scholarship, but there aren't enough scholarships for everybody. We compete in the workplace, but not everybody who wants the promotion gets it. We compete for public office, whether it's for president of the United States or Jefferson Central High student council representative. We compete in the business world—Pepsi wants you to drink Pepsi and Coke wants you to drink Coke.

These are legitimate—in some ways, necessary—arenas of competition. But in other arenas of life, competition is like vinegar poured on a chocolate sundae. It doesn't belong there, and it ruins things. Vinegar belongs in salad dressing, not on ice cream.

Popularity is an arena like this. There's nothing wrong with enjoying popularity if you have it just by being you, nor is there anything wrong with wanting to be liked and admired for good reasons. But deliberately trying to win more admirers than someone else, deliberately trying to gather more friends (or people who pretend to be) than someone else...that's like pouring lots of vinegar over the ice cream.

So is knocking yourself out to be somebody's girlfriend or boyfriend and winning out over a competitor. Sure, lots of movies have been based on this concept, and some of them have been genuinely funny, but in real life it's more often ugly than funny.

Having a relationship should come from being *chosen,* not from pushing buttons to make it happen, and the other person should be...a *person,* not a trophy won against competition. (Besides, will he or she still like you when you've stopped competing so hard and settled down to being regular old you?)

Unofficially competing with others to see who can own the most stuff, whether it's clothes or gadgets or whatever, doesn't prove anything either. In the end, it's just your *stuff.* It's not *you*

Competition in an arena in which it belongs is good when it leads you to become a better person, the best that you can be, whether it's point guard or first chair of the bassoon section or captain of the debate team. It's good if it leads you to sharpen your skills, reach, grow, and achieve. You can do all those things, by the way, even if you don't end up at the very top of the list. You've still benefited from competition.

Obviously competition is not good if it leads you to use shortcuts, such as cheating, lying, or using energy-enhancing drugs, to put yourself ahead of your competitors. It's not good if it leads you to think that you're a better person than someone you have surpassed in a particular field.

Competition is good if it ends when the event is over. It's not good when it creates ugliness afterward—fights and vandalism after a football game are some examples. (Granted, this is usually not the doing of the players themselves.)

Competition is good when it's *part* of life. It's not good when it *becomes* life. When the drive to win in a particular area overshadows and crowds out everything else (other responsibilities, relationships with family and friends, faith, relationship with God), then it becomes a false god in itself.

Competition is good when it's appropriate for the age of the competitors and bad when it isn't. A regional basketball playoff between twelve-year-olds is not an event that will alter the fate of the universe.

"Know yourself," Socrates said long ago. Examining how you approach and respond to competition can be a step toward doing that. Here are some possibilities.

1. *Competition is everything.* Being first or close to it in the cafeteria line at school approaches the same level

of importance as winning the 400-meter dash at the state track meet. This is competition gone over the edge. It frequently puts the competitor in a foul mood when he or she doesn't win. And it can lead to losing friends who get tired of always being edged out or simply being part of a contest.

2. *Sounds like fun—bring it on.* These individuals love to compete when the possibility of the challenge is offered. Winning is definitely their goal, but they're not destroyed if it doesn't happen. The key ideas are action, effort, and fun. It can get pretty serious when the competition has high stakes, as in a regional or state finals event. But it still doesn't *become* life. People in this group can deal with the results, win or lose.

3. *But what if...?* Sometimes people avoid competition due to anxiety over the possibility of not performing well. They don't have an irrational need to win, but they're afraid of looking bad, at least as they imagine it. People here need to remember that no individual activity *defines* you as a person. Maybe you dance with all the fluid grace of an elephant. (Dancing is not usually a competition, but it is open to comparisons of ability.) Hey, if you enjoy it and your date wants to dance, then dance.

4. *Not me.* Some people simply prefer to do many things alone, including developing and exercising new skills. They just don't like a crowd watching or even knowing about it. That's okay, as long as it's a choice, not a reaction to fear.

5. *Will I have to do much or move a lot?* Some people

don't like to compete in anything because they don't like to do *anything* or move anything very much—their legs, their arms, their brain, their position in front of the TV... They avoid competition because it usually involves the terribly unpleasant element of work. Well, it's okay if they never join a soccer team or play in a chess tournament. That's their choice. But fulfilling necessary responsibilities and obligations in life is not a choice.

Maybe intense competition stirs your blood like few other things. Maybe you agree with Vince Lombardi, a firm Catholic and one of the greatest football coaches of all time: "I believe in God, and I believe in human decency. I also believe that any man's finest hour...is that moment when he has worked his heart out in a good cause and lies exhausted on the field of battle—victorious."

Maybe you believe that a man or a woman can have his or her finest hour without ever stepping onto a field of battle of any kind. That's fine, too.

Or perhaps you believe that the most important fields of battle are private ones, where the opponent is one's own self, as when someone fights and overcomes an addiction or a powerful temptation.

That's all okay. We don't have to be alike. Competition of any kind doesn't have to be the same kind of value for all of us. But being a follower of Jesus—that needs to be *the* value, and it needs to direct whatever approach to competition we have.

Words From the Word

Athletes exercise self-control in all things; they do it to receive a perishable wreath, but we an imperishable one. So I do not run aimlessly, nor do I box as though beating the air.

—1 Corinthians 9:25–26

Whatever you do, in word or deed, do everything in the name of the Lord Jesus, giving thanks to God the Father through him.

—Colossians 3:17

Other Voices

Let's use competition as a benchmark to measure ourselves against, but let's stop competing over boyfriends, girlfriends, status, friends, popularity, positions, attention, and the like—and start enjoying life.

—Sean Covey, from The 7 Habits of Highly Effective Teens

If it doesn't matter who wins or loses, then why do they keep score?

—Vince Lombardi

I'm not in competition with anybody but myself. My goal is to beat my last performance.

—Celine Dion

Bottom Line

Competition—in arenas where it belongs—is good when it leads you to become a better person than you were. It's good when it's *part* of life. It's not good when it *becomes* life. And it's okay if you like competition a lot or like it very little.

NINE

Acceptance: Sometimes, Not Always

Take care not to make a covenant with the inhabitants of the land to which you are going, or it will become a snare among you.

−Exodus 34:12

They're from outer space! They don't look like us! They have a third eye in the middle of their foreheads! Obviously, they're evil and dangerous! Call out the Army! Drop some bombs on them before they destroy us!

A lot of old sci-fi movies and stories revolved around that unthinking reaction. Visitors from space dropped in on planet Earth, earthlings assumed they were bad guys, it got ugly from there on, and only at the end did we realize, perhaps too late, that they were really pretty nice and had come in peace.

If only we earthlings had been more accepting of differences...

Acceptance. You hear about it from preschool ("Now, you know, girls and boys, we're not all alike, and that's good—we need to *accept* one another") to college orientation ("Our university prides itself on the diversity of its student body and fosters mutual acceptance of that enriching diversity"). Side by side with "acceptance" is "tolerance." Although a dictionary would give slightly differing definitions, in terms of behavior they amount to almost the same thing.

Acceptance and tolerance: good things?

Usually. Not always.

Depends on what you're accepting and tolerating.

Usually acceptance and tolerance are great. They indicate that we are free of prejudice; that we do not put down others' views, beliefs, and practices that differ from our own; that we accept people who are racially, politically, religiously, or culturally different.

We could use tons more of acceptance and tolerance... correctly understood. Our world has seen too many cases of *in*tolerance. Intolerance says, "You are not like us— therefore we will destroy you, or enslave you, or at least consider ourselves superior to you and try to make your life miserable."

But acceptance and tolerance do not mean our brains go into some kind of slushy neutral and stop working. They don't mean we walk around saying, "That's cool— whatever" about almost anything and everything. They don't mean that anybody's idea or opinion is just as good and acceptable as anybody else's opinion. That's nuts. It might work if you're talking about which laundry detergent works best, but it's not true about everything in life.

For example: You have a horrible pain in your stomach that won't go away. Whose opinion do you want: that of a classmate who got a B+ in biology or that of a doctor?

A relative has just left you a hundred thousand dollars, which—if invested wisely—will make your financial future a lot easier. Whose opinion do you want: that of a friend who keeps hoping to win the lottery or that of a professional investment counselor?

In this country, everyone has an equal right to have an opinion and, usually, to voice it. That's great. That's not the case in most of the world. But are all opinions, *all messages*, equally valid, true, worthwhile, and acceptable?

Is doing a research paper just as much fun as a pool party? Someone *might* have that opinion, you know.

We're constantly on the receiving end of messages, even though we don't always realize it. Every time we look at a billboard or a magazine advertisement, for example, we're receiving a message, and usually more than one. One message is about the product. But often there's another one that, at least indirectly, says something about life, about people, about how to act.

And sometimes that message is just plain wrong.

A few years ago, a van manufacturer ran a series of ads in youth-oriented magazines. The ads always featured a young guy and girl either in the van or about to enter it. The caption on the ad read, "What a great way to get to know someone!"

An attempt to sell vans? Sure, but it said a lot more than that.

Riding in a van has nothing to do with getting to know another person, other than perhaps discovering whether or not that person is subject to motion sickness. At least indirectly, the message was "Sex is a great way to get to know someone," therefore, "Sex with someone you're interested in is okay," and then the conclusion: "Our van can give you a mobile, private place in which to do it."

We twenty-first century Christians aren't the only ones surrounded by very un-Christian messages. So were the first-century Corinthians. That's one of the reasons Paul wrote his first letter to them.

In Corinth, pagan messages flurried around like dust particles in the air. Some Corinthian Christians had shifted their brains into neutral and had more or less accepted these messages. They had convinced themselves, for example, that they could be followers of Jesus and still have sex with anyone who looked interesting, or acknowledge a pagan idol now and then.

Paul wrote to straighten them out, to put their brains back in gear, to get them thinking again in a Christian way. He didn't expect them to hide away in a cave somewhere, safe from temptation. Corinth was their home, and they had to live there. Paul didn't expect them to make war on any kind of non-Christians, either. But he emphatically said, *Think! You're Christians. You cannot accept and blend in with everything that's going on around you!*

That's true of us today. Accepting people, including those who are quite different in their beliefs, is part of being a Christian. Accepting any message they send is *not*. We Christians cannot say, "Oh, well...whatever..." to any message that comes our way. If we do, we should call ourselves Whatevers, not Christians.

As Christians, we need to look beneath the surface of advertisements, music videos, television shows, movies. We need to listen to lyrics with our brains and our morals working. What do these things say about how to live? What do they say is important in life? What do they say about relationships, love, sex, marriage, money, pleasure, and power?

Whenever we connect with the culture we live in, we need to ask some questions: What is this saying? Who's saying it? Do they have any qualifications in this area? Do they have anything to gain by saying it? *How does it measure up against what Jesus taught?*

We also need to ask whether an idea is acceptable just because it's cleverly written about or cleverly acted out. Is something okay because it gets a laugh from a theater full of people or a room full of television viewers?

Laughing is one of the best things we do as human beings—usually. It's often a sign that life is going well and that people are enjoying one another's company. But it can be deceptive if we get caught up into the brainless variety of acceptance and tolerance. We can slide into thinking that *whatever prompts laughter must be sort of okay,* or at least not very seriously wrong.

I've asked more than one student how they could approve of or be part of certain pieces of pretty awful entertainment that were totally at war with Christian standards. I often got the explanation, *"But it's funny!"* I usually responded, "Think about what you just said. What if someone thought that making you feel miserable was funny? What if they did it really creatively and cleverly? Would that make it okay?" (I resisted the temptation to say, "Grow a brain.")

A few years ago, a lot of people laughed themselves silly over a movie about four guys who had made a resolution to lose their virginity by prom night. Undoubtedly some of the dialogue was humorous and some of the acting clever. But how many people left the theaters coming a notch or two closer to thinking, *Well, that's not so bad—you have to lose it sometime?*

Losing virginity *just to say you've done it…*with whomever doesn't matter…*that's okay?*

"But it was *funny!*"

What if it were your sister or your future daughter in real life who got hit on by a guy who simply decided it was time to have sex with somebody/anybody—would it still be funny then?

This leads to another question: Is an idea okay because it's "just a show" or "just a song" or "just a story"? Those words come spilling out all the time, and it's easy once again to put the Christian brain into slushy neutral and use those words to accept or excuse things that are just plain simply wrong.

What about a show or a rap or a video game that depicts people, including children, being beaten up, tortured, and raped?

Remember, it's "just a show."

If you say "no," then you agree that some things are or should be off limits by their nature because they're *just too wrong* to be passed off as entertainment.

And the above example certainly can't be the only one.

Is a piece of entertainment okay simply because it presents "what happens these days?" That's the justification for a lot of rap lyrics. ("Hey, it's part of the culture.")

Yes, rape and treating women as though they are toys to be used up and thrown away happens. I guess you could call it "part of the culture" in some places if you want to grossly violate the word "culture." Murder, violence, and rampant drug use also happen. They're part of all too many scenes and "cultures." Does that mean it's okay to produce entertainment that makes them sound normal—and even exciting? (Or "funny!")

We need to learn acceptance and tolerance, all right. But not about everything. That turns us into unthinking sponges that soak up every message anybody sends us. If Paul were writing to the Corinthians today, he might say, "Remember that you are Christians. Christians are not unthinking sponges that blend in with everything they see and hear."

Words From the Word

You shall not do as they do in the land of Egypt, where you lived, and you shall not do as they do in the land of Canaan, to which I am bringing you.

–*Leviticus 18:3*

Do not be conformed to this world, but be transformed by the renewing of your minds, so that you may discern what is the will of God—what is good and acceptable and perfect.

–*Romans 12:2*

Other Voices

Coming to your senses means trusting that if something stinks, you should not go near it.

–*Pastor William R. Grimbol*

You start to think "It's all okay." But it's not. I found that out. Wish I'd found it out sooner.

–*Former student*

Bottom Line

Accepting—and loving—other *people* is a Christian ideal. Accepting and blending in with all messages and all the "culture" in the world around us indicates a Christian brain lapsing into slushy neutral.

TEN

No! Absolutely Not! *Never!*

No testing has overtaken you that is not common to everyone. God is faithful, and he will not let you be tested beyond your strength, but with the testing, he will also provide the way out so that you may be able to endure it.

–1 Corinthians 10:13

How about an extra worksheet on irregular verb usage?" I asked my class one afternoon when we had a little extra time to spare. They stared at me blankly.

"Oh, come on," I said. "What are you afraid of? Just one never hurt anybody. It's cool—you'll like it."

They glared at me. They didn't budge. Their ability to just say no was stunning. Of course, we were talking about irregular verb usage practice sheets.

That's not exactly high on the list of enticing, attractive, tempting items that could screw up your life. In fact, it's not even on the list.

But the list is full of other things, and we all know exactly what they are. How do you avoid them when the opportunity to do them drops into your life, often aided by a good bit of peer pressure?

Well, hey, it's simple—remember? You "just say no." Just say no, just say no, just say no, just say no, just say no, just say no...

You've probably heard that advice often enough to get *really* tired of hearing it. It can even be irritating because it seems to turn the job of refusing to do something into a simple act of button pushing. Just say no, and both the temptation and the pressure disappear, everybody is off your case, and all is cool.

Problem is, saying no really *is* the only refusal skill. There's not a whole set of "refusal skills." There's one: saying no. And it really *is simple.* Say no. You can get it down to one word, one syllable.

But "simple" is not "easy." When I instruct first-time racquetball players, I tell them that the rules are really very simple, and they're glad to hear that. About a half hour later, however, they sometimes protest, "I thought you said this was simple."

"I said the rules are simple. I didn't same the game was easy."

Here are some suggestions that might help make the *very simple but very difficult* task of saying no a little smoother.

Saying no starts long before you need to say it to someone. If you don't say it to yourself, you'll probably never say it to someone else. It begins when you're alone and thinking about yourself, your life, your future. Your "no" starts before you leave the house, before you go on a date, before you go to a party, before you just hang out, before you join any group of people. If it doesn't start long before those things, it probably won't happen.

The best way to prepare your "no" is to make a list of things you will not do—no exceptions. You can make it in your mind, but putting it in writing is more effective than just letting it float around in your head. It helps to actually see it.

A lot of basically good people make mistakes because they have never made a deliberate, conscious decision about things they would never do. They didn't make a list—or didn't really commit to what was on it.

"I will never rob a bank, sell military secrets to nations that don't like us, or try to overthrow the government." Nice start, but then we need to get more practical.

It's not going to be a terribly long list because the topics, as we said, are no great mystery. When young peoples' lives get messed up, what's involved? No secret, no mystery. Alcohol, other drugs, sex, violence, vandalism, theft. We could add a few additional, somewhat less likely items, such as gambling, but 90 percent of the problems are right there in that last sentence.

When drug use, premarital sex, or violent activity come back to bite, few people think, "Gosh, I figured that stuff was totally safe!"

What they did think was, "I can beat the odds. I can keep it under control. I can dodge the bullet. It might mess up other people who aren't cool about it, but it won't come back to bite me."

The key to the "things I will not do" list is the "no exceptions." As soon as you begin to add, "Well...the *only* way I might *ever* _____ is if _____," you're practically setting it up to happen because the "only if" part is very likely to come around, or at least appear to.

Absolutely classic example: "The *only* way I would *ever* have sex is if I *really loved* that person and I *knew for certain* that he/she loved me."

How often have we seen that scenario blow up in a million shattered emotional pieces? Following is an example, and I never make up examples. This happened.

One afternoon I talked with a former student who had been having sex with his girlfriend because he was positive that all those "only if" conditions were true. *Four hours* after they had sex (for the last time), his girlfriend told him that she was really in love with someone else, and that they needed to end the relationship.

Making your "never" list is a start. Now you've got to make it work under pressure, especially pressure from others.

You have to be convinced of two things. (1) You have a right to live by your list, by standards you set, and no peer or group of peers should pressure you to do otherwise. (2) You do not owe anyone an explanation or a reason for your "no." Your decision to act in a way that's good for your life and your future is the only reason you need.

One classic technique that you can use used to be called the "broken record" technique. I'm not sure what they call it now because a lot of young people don't know how records used to operate.

Back in nearly cave-person days, people used to listen to music on those ancient round black discs called records. Sometimes the needle would get stuck in a groove and you would hear the same few words over and over ("I love you bay-yay—love you bay-yay—love you bay-yay…").

Broken-record method of saying no sounds like this:

"Why aren't you coming with us."

"Because we all know what's going to happen, and I don't do that stuff."

"Why not."

"Because I don't do that stuff."

"What's your stupid *reason*, man?"

"You just heard it. I don't do that stuff."

"Never thought you'd be such a jerk." (You'll probably hear something different and stronger than "jerk.")

"I'm not. I just don't do that stuff."

Sometimes you can mix in a little agreeing-without-really-agreeing. It sounds like this.

"Man, you're really a %*#$@$#% jerk."

"I can see you *think* I am. I still don't do that stuff."

"You know, you're really starting to &^%$#* me off!"

"Yeah, I can see that."

"You're gonna regret this."

"I can see you feel that way."

The broken record is beautifully simple, but again not easy. The trick is not to get sucked into feeling that you have to come up with reasons—and not to make counter-accusations of your own. It's a wonderful combination of (a) not giving in an inch, and (b) not fighting back. You become like a master martial artist who dodges every blow without ever throwing one. After a while, the other person feels like he or she is trying to fight the air. The air never gives in and it never fights back—which means *the air wins.*

Learn to recognize things that people often use to pressure others. Often they're very good things—friendship, loyalty, strength, community, success. But even good things can be manipulated for purposes for which they were never intended. A beautiful vase can be used to knock someone out, and a diamond necklace can be used to strangle someone.

You may hear things like: "I thought we were friends." "Friends are supposed to stick together." "I'd do it for *you* if *you* asked me to." "Come *on*—I'm [or "we're"] *counting on* you!"

They're all intended to make you feel guilty—guilty that you're not being a true friend, that you're being disloyal or unworthy of someone's friendship. They're all lies, of course, because true friends respect one another's freedom and right to make decisions about how to act.

Friends should be able to count on one another for things that are good and needed, even when it's tough to do. But when Jesus talked about loving someone enough to lay down your life for that person, he did not mean being willing to risk getting arrested so a friend has a companion or at least a lookout while committing a crime.

Giving in to people who pressure you to do something wrong, harmful to yourself, or against your wishes in any way is a no-win situation. You may more or less succeed in keeping the peace and getting people off your case. But you end up disliking everyone involved—the person or people who didn't respect you enough to honor your wishes, and yourself for being weak and giving in to them.

Jesus had a better idea, and he lived it himself. When he was tempted in the desert, he simply stood there and said "No!" several times—even though they hadn't invented records yet. But he obviously had made a list.

Words From the Word

Now Joseph was handsome and good-looking. And after a time, his master's wife cast her eyes on Joseph and said, "Lie with me." But he refused. And although she spoke to Joseph day after day, he would not consent to lie beside her or to be with her.

–Genesis 39:6–7, 10

The tempter came and said to him, "If you are the Son of God, command these stones to become loaves of bread."

–Matthew 4:3

Other Voices

I hope you make a lot of nice friends out there /
But just remember there's a lot of bad and beware.

–Cat Stevens

Seems there's always someone trying to push you
to do something.

–Phil Collins

Bottom Line

There's really only one way to say no: Say no. It's immensely simple—and often very difficult. But when you give in to pressure to do something wrong that you don't want, everybody loses…and you end up disliking everybody, including yourself.

ELEVEN

Putting the Good in Good-Bye

There was much weeping among them all; they embraced Paul and kissed him, grieving especially because of what he had said, that they would not see him again. Then they brought him down to the ship.

–Acts 20:37–38

"M ust you go, darling?" Samantha asked, her voice softly trembling like the softly trembling call of a delicate bird whose fragile heart was about to break. Her lips quivered with tremors of emotion that swelled up from deep within her anguished heart. She was starting to cry like crazy, too.

Alexander turned quickly and crossed the room with long, firm strides. Ever more quickly he strode, until at last he clasped her in his muscular, sinewy arms and held her close.

"I was all the way across the room and couldn't hear you worth a darn," he said with deep emotion, gazing into her tear-filled eyes. "But I know that you spoke words that, once repeated by your soft velvet lips, shall be treasured by me for as long as my heart shall beat. What fair words did you speak, my love?"

"Do you really gotta go, hunkypunkins?" Samantha repeated.

"Yes," Alexander replied after a pause, his voice also beginning to tremble. Rugged man though he was, he too knew the meaning of heartache. "Darling, a man can live a thousand lifetimes and never win Super Bowl tickets. When he receives such a call, he must follow his destiny."

Once in a while, I get the notion to practice writing a romance novel. I don't know whether Samantha and Alexander will survive this farewell, but saying good-bye is one of the most common things we do. In one form or another, we will say good-bye well over a half million times in our lives. If our job involves talking with customers or clients, it may exceed two million.

We usually don't think about it very much and for good reason because most good-byes are not big ones. We write "C-ya" at the end of e-mails or Ims. We say "talk to you later" or just "later" at the end of phone conversations, and there's nothing big involved.

But some good-byes are much bigger than that. They signal the end of a period in our lives and often the beginning of another very different one. They include good-byes to classmates and teachers at graduation, good-byes to family and friends as we leave for college or the military, good-byes to coworkers as we leave one job for another.

Some good-byes are permanent and usually very sad or painful, such as the death of a relative or friend, or the end of a relationship that has been broken beyond repair. Other good-byes fall somewhere between routine and major, such as saying good-bye to friends or relatives we've visited and won't see again for quite a while.

Sometimes we also say good-bye to a lifestyle or an era in our lives, instead of to a person. That can be painful, frightening, and filled with hope all at the same time— as when a person turns his or her back on an addiction and begins the journey toward recovery. At other times, we're not even aware that we're saying good-bye, as when a young woman or man shoulders full responsibility for a major decision or a challenging obligation—and in doing so, says good-bye to any remainder of childhood, where most things just get done for you.

All of these situations can be times of grace, which is a way of saying they can be filled with God's presence, with God's working in our lives to make something good happen. Answering God's call often means saying good-bye to people we love and have grown close to.

Paul experienced this many times on his missionary journeys. Jesus and his apostles experienced separation because of the mission Jesus had been sent to fulfill. At the Last Supper, Jesus told them, "Because I have said these things to you, sorrow has filled your hearts. Nevertheless, I tell you the truth: it is to your advantage that I go away, for if I do not go away, the Advocate will not come to you; but if I go, I will send him to you" (Jn 16:6–7).

Since we say good-bye so often, let's think about ways in which we can make them more meaningful, learn from them, and receive the grace that's in them.

Asking what we've learned from the good-byes we've said may seem like the classic question, "What did you learn in school today?" to which the classic answer is, "Nothing." That may be literally true in some school cases, but it usually means, "Nothing I found very interesting" or "Nothing I want to talk about right now because I'm watching a good cartoon."

With some effort, however, most people could list a number of things they had learned. Even studying the climate of the Sahara Desert can make a person appreciate the weather in Cleveland a lot more.

Lessons from our good-byes can be like that. What were the gifts? What were the inspirations? How have we changed and grown? Those may sound like heavy questions that you address in a retreat-like setting with lots of meditative silence. Not really. This reflection often takes only a few moments.

I'll give you a couple examples that I've thought of from my own life.

A couple summers ago, I had lunch with a kid who was about to move to a different city, attend a different school, and live with his other parent and different people. It had been a difficult and scary decision, but as we sat at a restaurant table, he said simply, "I'm happy. I hope everybody else will be happy too."

After lunch, I said good-bye and good luck, all the usual things, and on the surface, that was it. I had taken a kid that I probably wouldn't see again (and haven't) to lunch. But it was really more than that. I had been given an example of courage in making a difficult decision and then being at peace with it, in spite of not knowing how things were going to turn out. Pretty good lesson from a young teen to an adult over four times his age. Maybe I should be more at peace with my own decisions. Maybe I should not be so reluctant to take risks.

Not too long ago, I said good-bye to a number of people at an adult day-care center. We had gone there to help serve lunch and provide some companionship. I would have been foolish simply to drive home without having learned anything from the people I had said good-bye to.

Bev had taught me that it's possible to laugh—very often and *very* loudly—in spite of being in pain. Jack had taught me that it's possible to be good-natured and to enjoy life in spite of being weak and nearly helpless.

Both those good-byes came at the end of perhaps three hours. Reflecting on the lessons and gifts of a much longer time together can yield a wealth of treasure.

We can't live in the past, but it's a shame to waste it. Never thinking about it makes it impossible to learn from it, and it's the only part of our lives we really *can* learn from.

Besides learning from our good-byes, we should be

grateful for the people and the times we've said good-bye to. I give thanks for Bev, thanks for Jack, thanks for my lunch companion Jordan. Those are just three recent ones from my life. You could make a long list in spite of having lived probably less than two decades.

Things like "Thanks also for my childhood." Millions of kids, because of poverty, slavery, or war never have one. "Thanks for my high school years." They may not have been perfect, but some kids never get that far.

Think of the people who have moved in and out of the landscape of your life and be grateful for them. "Thanks for Mrs. Kramer, who gave me my first job." "Thanks for my baby-sitter, Sheila, who first got me interested in art." "Thanks for Mr. Reilly, who made me believe I could play soccer well."

Would you like to return the gift that these people have been to you? You can do that in a couple of ways. One is by praying for them. In fact, the actual meaning of expressions of farewell in many languages is a hope for a person's closeness to God.

"Good-bye" itself is a condensed version of "God be with you." The Spanish *"adios,"* the Italian *"addio,"* the Portuguese *"adeus,"* and the French *"adieu"* all mean "toward God." Spanish has an even fuller version: *"Vaya con Dios:"* "May you go with God."

So pray for that camp counselor who calmed you down and made you feel okay when you were a scared-to-death eight-year-old. It may have been years since you said good-bye to him or her, but that's okay. Even if he or she now resides in That Great Summer Camp in the

Sky, God will respond to your prayer on behalf of someone else that person loves or who needs prayer.

Pray for the first person you had a crush on. (Roberta Orf, second grade. *Vaya con Dios*, Roberta.) Pray for the people you met on vacation whom you wished lived closer to you so you could get to know one another better. Pray for friends from past years whom you never formally said good-bye to, but wish you had before you went your separate ways.

Enrich good-byes. Celebrate them. One of the best ways to do this is with a written note, letter, or card. No matter how convenient e-mail is, it will never carry the weight of a hand-written note or letter that says, "Thanks for the memories; thanks for who you've been to me." It takes a few minutes and a stamp. It doesn't have to be fancy. Now if you want to create a visually stunning card with state-of-the-art computer graphics, that's fine, and your effort in doing so will be a statement of your caring. But a simple handwritten note will have an effect far beyond its simple appearance.

Send one to Grandma after you've returned from a visit. Send one to friends who have moved away. Send one to one of your favorite teachers from past years. Send one to the coach at the end of the season. (Note to guys who may find this more alien and difficult than girls do: It doesn't have to be mushy, okay? "Thanks for a great year—you were cool" will work just fine.)

Good-byes are moments of grace for both you and the person you're saying farewell to. Don't miss the grace. Spread it around.

Alexander stood at the door. Samantha stood at the window, dabbing her tear-laden eyes with an exquisite, lace-edged handkerchief. "Think of me...at least during half-time," she said, her voice trembling with grief. Once again, Alexander was quickly by her side.

"I was all the way across the room again, my love," he said with deep emotion.

Words From the Word

And remember, I am with you always, to the end of the world.

–Matthew 28:20

When she could hide him [the infant Moses] no longer she got a papyrus basket for him...she put the child in it and placed it among the reeds on the bank of the river.

–Exodus 2:3–4

[David and Jonathan] ...wept with each other; David wept the more. Then Jonathan said to David, "Go in peace, since both of us have sworn in the name of the LORD...." He got up and left; and Jonathan went into the city.

–1 Samuel 20:41–42

Other Voices

Good night, good night! Parting is such sweet sorrow, / That I shall say good night till it be morrow.
–William Shakespeare, Romeo and Juliet

Every good-bye ain't gone.
–South Carolina proverb

Near, far, wherever you are / I believe that the heart does go on.
–Love theme from Titanic

Bottom Line

"Good-bye" or some form of it is one of the most common things we say. Although many "good-bye moments" are routine, many others are rich with things to learn, rich with things and people to be grateful for...rich with God's grace.

TWELVE

What Matters to You?

In the beginning, we said that strategies for life have a lot to do with what's important to you—those things sometimes called values.

I just got back from an errand to the supermarket an hour ago. For real—it's not just a made-up example. Among other things, I bought a tube of toothpaste on sale for $2.50 instead of its usual price of $3.99 (or "a $3.99 value"). You could say I got an extra $1.49 worth of value for free, compliments of the nice folks who run the supermarket chain.

And there was a cantaloupe on sale for $1.50, when it's usually $2.00—or so the sign said above the bin of cantaloupes. An extra fifty cents of value...for free! In advertising, this is called "shopping for values." It's supposed to be a smart consumer strategy.

A couple weeks ago, my wife and I watched an infomercial video that came free in the mail, advertising an indoor swimming pool. (I guess it was a slow evening; it has to be a slow evening when you watch an infomercial.) According to the video, if we acted quickly, we could get an incredible deal on this pool—a couple thousand dollars or so off the regular price. And supposedly, this bin of water in our home would transform our lives. We would be just like the people in the video— happy, fulfilled, and wearing huge, gosh-I'm-having-fun! grins on our faces every day.

It's not a nasty-by-nature idea by itself (although I should weigh the cost of that luxury against what it could do for impoverished people). It would be nice to stretch out on the surface of right-in-the-home, temperature-controlled water after I finish…well, for example, after I finish writing this final chapter. And it would be fun to invite other people over to admire and use this large gadget. ("Hey, Dave and Gloria, bring your swim suits! Yeah, I know it's December, but you'll need them—wait till you see what we just got!")

Problem is, we'd have to pay for the huge *remainder* of the "bargain," the part that wasn't discounted. Sure, we could put it on a credit card, but making the payments would interfere with other things that are more important—like being able to pay all the normal bills. Making sure we don't financially sink seemed like a better strategy than buying a luxury in which we could float.

Bought the toothpaste and the cantaloupe. Didn't buy the pool.

Toothpaste and the cantaloupe seem pretty ordinary. But underneath the toothpaste is dental health, which is pretty important, even if it's ordinary. The cantaloupe? Well, my wife likes to take some fresh fruit with her to work in the morning. Getting it, preparing it, and putting it in a little plastic bag is one way I tell her that I love her. That *is* important.

Life is kind of like that. The really important things that we usually put on the list of "Things That Really Matter"—God, faith, family, love, friendship, being true to ourselves, and so on—are often lived out in little packages like toothpaste and cantaloupe.

Other things sometimes seem glitzier and more exciting. Like the pool. Or like temporary social success and status, short-lived excitement, and pleasures of one kind or another. Looking cool, feeling cool. At the time, they *seem* or *feel* more important, even though we would never *say* they are. And so, it's tempting to give them a lot more time than we give to the things we put on our "Really Important" list.

Sometimes, like the pool, they're not wrong. They just probably won't deliver the nonstop, apparent happiness they claim to bring. At other times—at least in the way we're tempted to get them—they really *are* wrong. Just plain wrong.

What's really important to you? How much time are you giving it?

As you may have heard once or twice before, only you can make those decisions. So make them...ahead of time. Before you get in situations where you will have to act on them or not act on them.

The alternative, as we noted in the Introduction, is living the line from "Bohemian Rhapsody:" "Any way the wind blows..."

You want to be more in charge than that.

The best way to make sure you're in charge of your life in a good way is to keep checking in with God who, in the end, really *is* in charge of everything.

Best wishes. Hang in.

Appendix of Prayers

Two Mirrors

I look in a mirror every morning, Lord,
    and usually several other times a day.
Check to make sure my face is on straight,
    that kind of stuff.
Sometimes I'm happy with what I see,
    well, more or less, sort of,
      and sometimes I wish it were better.
But at least I look in the mirror.
There's another mirror that I sometimes avoid,
    the one that shows the inside of me.
If the outside mirror shows a blotch on my face
    or that my hair is stupid,
      I know it will eventually go away or be fixable.
I'm less sure of the blotches and the stupid stuff
    on the inside of me;
      so sometimes I don't look
      for days at a time.

Help me look in the inside mirror, Lord,
   and trust that you can heal
   whatever isn't right there.
And then help me
   let you do that.

Honey and Vinegar

Somebody said something today
   that made me feel great.
They meant it and it was real;
   it was about something good about me.
I'd like to think it was *you* talking to me.
Okay, I'll trust that it *was* you talking to me.
In return, *I* should be *you* to someone else
   and say something like that to another person...
   something true and comforting and uplifting.
Help me find that person—no,
   help me find several persons
   and the true and right words to say.
Of course, not everybody tells me nice
   and comforting things;
   sometimes people say hurtful things.
And sometimes—I'm ashamed of this—
   I pass those along, too,
   sometimes back to that same person
   and sometimes to others.

With your help, I'd like to do only the first kind.
Help me pass along the honey but let the vinegar
    splash off and dry up;
      because the vinegar is not you talking
      either to me or through me.

Toxic Dust

I have this problem with the world I live in.
Not the planet in general but
    my specific young person's culture—
    the music, the cable TV, the clothes, the customs,
    the things older people roll their eyeballs over
    and complain about
    and warn me about.
They're afraid it will lead me to think the wrong way
    and do wrong things.
They're afraid that if I walk around in it
    I'll pick up some of it—
    kind of like getting dust on your skin
    just by going outside.
I'm not stupid, Lord.
I know our entertainment culture glorifies
    some wrong things.
But a lot of it is exciting and fun,
    and being a part of it makes me feel I fit in.
I need some help dealing with it:
    separating the okay
    from the probably not so good
    from the definitely wrong, bad, and awful.

At times, for whatever reasons, I have a hard time
   telling which is which...or maybe
   sometimes I would rather not know.
At those times, I really need you.

Heavy Back Pack

Sometimes my backpack, full of books and other stuff
   that I need to do what I have to do,
   feels overloaded; too full; unfairly heavy.
And when it does,
   sometimes I think it's a symbol of my life.
   Too much stuff going on;
   too many demands on time.
People talk and write about all the stress
   in young people's lives,
   and how they'd like to take us back
   to simpler times
   when a young person's life wasn't so full
   and organized.
And on the other hand they talk and write about
   how easy young people have it today...
   all the advantages, privileges,
   communication devices,
   the cool stuff I take for granted, I guess.
But, you know, Lord, I can't figure out who is right
   about us in general
and about me in particular.

When I feel I'm on overload,
  is it real and I need to change something,
  or am I just being a little lazy
  and feeling sorry for myself?
I could use some help sorting this out and
  responding the way you want me to.

The School Door

School doors have a heavy spring; pulled open,
  they don't stay open very long
  before they slam shut,
  unless they're held open for the next person.
Some people squirt through a brief opening
  left over from the person ahead, and
  let the door close behind them.
Others hold the door for the person behind them.
  I've done both, Lord.
Good manners and bad manners—
  I've had them both.
But I want to hold the door for someone
  more often from now on.
And do and say similar things—
  it's not just the school doors.
Because I know that a little bit of courtesy
  in any of many, many ways
  brings a little bit of you—
  and perhaps more of you
  than it appears at the time.

The Rock and the Silly Putty

When I was young, I used to play with Silly Putty
and look at pebbles, little rocks with pretty colors
that came even more alive when they were wet.
And sometimes (don't tell my peers) I still do;
or if I don't, maybe I should...you know—
all that stuff about keeping simple wonder alive.
Back then,
I never thought that a rock and a glob of Silly Putty
would be symbols of how I have to
deal with my teenage, young adult life.
More often than I would like,
there's stuff I have to make a decision about.
And lots more often than I would like,
I have friends or things in general
Inviting me to stuff that's not so good.
Silly Putty is cool in its own way,
but I don't want to *be* it...
mindlessly melting and taking the shape
of whatever social container I'm in—
laughing at things I shouldn't laugh at,
seemingly agreeing with things
I shouldn't agree with.
Lord, help me be a rock when I need to be a rock,
keeping my own shape,
staying true to you
and to the me you want me to be.

Playstations and Play-Doh Praise the Lord

A lot of the Psalms
    call on things in creation to praise you, Lord:
    things like the heavens and the waters
    and the mountains and cedars,
    and that's all cool enough.
But I was thinking,
    I don't say a prayer of praise often enough.
Other prayers, yes,
    but not often enough a prayer of simple praise.
So, I'm going to use some things from today's world,
    my world,
    for a psalm of praise.
Hope you like it.

Diesel trucks, freight trains, and airplanes,
    sidewalks, soda pops, and Superglue,
    praise the Lord forever.
Playstations and Play-Doh,
    candy corn, popcorn, and corn on the cob,
    bless his name forever.
Cell phones, PDAs, Planners and scanners,
    CDs, DVDs, and cream cheese,
    sing the glory of the Lord.
Reese Cups, Seven-Ups, and little pups,
    ravioli, mostaccioli, and all that's holy
    announce his holy name.

E-mails, mall sales, and wagging tails,
    candy wrappers and non-nasty rappers,
    proclaim his marvelous works
    forever!

911

If you call 911,
    even if you can hardly speak,
    even if you aren't totally sure what your problem is,
    even if you think you're hopeless,
    they come and help you.
Sometimes I feel like I'm in a 911 situation,
    even if it's partly my imagination.
When that happens
    —and I'll try not to use this as an escape from
    being responsible for my life—
    if I can't think of fancy,
    situation-appropriate words to pray,
    can I please just pray
    "Almighty God, my Lord, Savior,
    and Helper...*911?*"
Actually, it may be just "Lord...911!"
Thanks.

Hand Wave Out the Back Window of the Departing Car

Some words are like "cool,"
    meaning they can mean a lot of things,
    depending on the situation, the time and place and
    whatever you're thinking and feeling at the time.
They can be said lovingly or sarcastically,
    with gratitude or with relief.
"Good-bye" is like that.
Sometimes I hate to say it,
    and sometimes I can't wait to say it,
    and sometimes I don't realize I've said it until later.
Good-bye's, whether temporary or permanent,
    are a part of life.
Help me make good ones, Lord.
Let me never say a brief, hurried, superficial good-bye
    to people who need to hear more than that,
    who need to know that I treasure and love them.
Let me never say a good-bye,
    especially a final one,
    without fully appreciating the gifts I've received
    from whoever or whatever I'm saying good-bye to,
    whether that's Grandma and Grandpa
    at the end of a Thanksgiving dinner
    or at their funeral Mass,
    or my school and my teachers
    and classmates at graduation,
    or even my childhood when things were simpler
    and easier to figure out.

Let me see all the good
   in the good people
   and good things I say good-bye to
   and realize that you were there in all of them.
And give me the courage to say good-bye
   to all the not-so-good things
   I really need to say good-bye to.